MAY 2005

RESUMES FOR

HIGH RS

VGM Professional Resumes Series

THIRD EDITION

RESUMES FOR

HIGH-TECH CAREERS

With Sample Cover Letters

The Editors of VGM Career Books

VGM Career Books

Chicago   New York   San Francisco   Lisbon   London   Madrid   Mexico City
Milan   New Delhi   San Juan   Seoul   Singapore   Sydney   Toronto

The **McGraw-Hill** Companies

Library of Congress Cataloging-in-Publication Data

Resumes for high tech careers / the editors of VGM Career Books.—3rd ed.
 p.   cm. — (VGM professional resumes series)
 ISBN 0-07-141155-0
 1. Resumes (Employment)   2. High technology industries—Vocational
guidance.   I. VGM Career Books (Firm)   II. Series.

HF5383.R44   2003
650.14'—2—dc21   2003050162

1 2 3 4 5 6 7 8 9 0   QPD/QPD   2 1 0 9 8 7 6 5 4 3

ISBN 0-07-141155-0

McGraw-Hill books are available at special quantity discounts to use as premiums and
sales promotions, or for use in corporate training programs. For more information, please
write to the Director of Special Sales, Professional Publishing, McGraw-Hill, Two Penn
Plaza, New York, NY 10121-2298. Or contact your local bookstore.

This book is printed on acid-free paper. 3269

Contents

Introduction

Your resume is a piece of paper (or an electronic document) that serves to introduce you to the people who will eventually hire you. To write a thoughtful resume, you must thoroughly assess your personality, your accomplishments, and the skills you have acquired. The act of composing and submitting a resume also requires you to carefully consider the company or individual that might hire you. What are they looking for, and how can you meet their needs? This book shows you how to organize your personal information and experience into a concise and well-written resume so that your qualifications and potential as an employee will be understood easily and quickly by a complete stranger.

Writing the resume is just one step in what can be a daunting job-search process, but it is an important element in the chain of events that will lead you to your new position. While you are probably a talented, bright, and charming person, your resume may not reflect these qualities. A poorly written resume can get you nowhere; a well-written resume can land you an interview and potentially a job. A good resume can even lead the interviewer to ask you questions that will allow you to talk about your strengths and highlight the skills you can bring to a prospective employer. Even a person with very little experience can find a good job if he or she is assisted by a thoughtful and polished resume.

Lengthy, typewritten resumes are a thing of the past. Today, employers do not have the time or the patience for verbose documents; they look for tightly composed, straightforward, action-based resumes. Although a one-page resume is the norm, a two-page resume may be warranted if you have had extensive job experience or have changed careers and truly need the space to properly position yourself. If, after careful editing, you still need more than one page to present yourself, it's acceptable to use a second page. A crowded resume that's hard to read would be the worst of your choices.

Distilling your work experience, education, and interests into such a small space requires preparation and thought. This book takes you step-by-step through the process of crafting an effective resume that will stand out in today's competitive marketplace. It serves as a workbook and a place to write down your experiences, while also including the techniques you'll need to pull all the necessary elements together. In the following pages, you'll find many examples of resumes that are specific to your area of interest. Study them for inspiration and find what appeals to you. There are a variety of ways to organize and present your information; inside, you'll find several that will be suitable to your needs. Good luck landing the job of your dreams!

The Elements of an Effective Resume

An effective resume is composed of information that employers are most interested in knowing about a prospective job applicant. This information is conveyed by a few essential elements. The following is a list of elements that are found in most resumes—some essential, some optional. Later in this chapter, we will further examine the role of each of these elements in the makeup of your resume.

- Heading

- Objective and/or Keyword Section

- Work Experience

- Education

- Honors

- Activities

- Certificates and Licenses

- Publications

- Professional Memberships

- Special Skills

- Personal Information

- References

The first step in preparing your resume is to gather information about yourself and your past accomplishments. Later you will refine this information, rewrite it using effective language, and organize it into an attractive layout. But first, let's take a look at each of these important elements individually so you can judge their appropriateness for your resume.

Heading

Although the heading may seem to be the simplest section of your resume, be careful not to take it lightly. It is the first section your prospective employer will see, and it contains the information she or he will need to contact you. At the very least, the heading must contain your name, your home address, and, of course, a phone number where you can be reached easily.

In today's high-tech world, many of us have multiple ways that we can be contacted. You may list your E-mail address if you are reasonably sure the employer makes use of this form of communication. Keep in mind, however, that others may have access to your E-mail messages if you send them from an account provided by your current company. If this is a concern, do not list your work E-mail address on your resume. If you are able to take calls at your current place of business, you should include your work number, because most employers will attempt to contact you during typical business hours.

If you have voice mail or a reliable answering machine at home or at work, list its number in the heading and make sure your greeting is professional and clear. Always include at least one phone number in your heading, even if it is a temporary number, where a prospective employer can leave a message.

You might have a dozen different ways to be contacted, but you do not need to list all of them. Confine your numbers or addresses to those that are the easiest for the prospective employer to use and the simplest for you to retrieve.

Objective

When seeking a specific career path, it is important to list a job or career objective on your resume. This statement helps employers know the direction you see yourself taking, so they can determine whether your goals are in line with those of their organization and the position available. Normally, an objective is one to two sentences long. Its contents will vary depending on your career field, goals, and personality. The objective can be specific or general, but it should always be to the point. See the sample resumes in this book for examples.

If you are planning to use this resume online, or you suspect your potential employer is likely to scan your resume, you will want to include a "keyword" in the objective. This allows a prospective employer, searching hundreds of resumes for a specific skill or position objective, to locate the keyword and find your resume. In essence, a keyword is what's "hot" in your particular field at a given time. It's a buzzword, a shorthand way of getting a particular message across at a glance. For example, if you are a lawyer, your objective might state your desire to work in the area of corporate litigation. In this case, someone searching for the keyword "corporate litigation" will pull up your resume and know that you want to plan, research, and present cases at trial on behalf of the corporation. If your objective states that you "desire a challenging position in systems design," the keyword is "systems design," an industry-specific shorthand way of saying that you want to be involved in assessing the need for, acquiring, and implementing high-technology systems. These are keywords and every industry has them, so it's becoming more and more important to include a few in your resume. (You may need to conduct additional research to make sure you know what keywords are most likely to be used in your desired industry, profession, or situation.)

There are many resume and job-search sites online. Like most things in the online world, they vary a great deal in quality. Use your discretion. If you plan to apply for jobs online or advertise your availability this way, you will want to design a scannable resume. This type of resume uses a format that can be easily scanned into a computer and added to a database. Scanning allows a prospective employer to use keywords to quickly review each applicant's experience and skills, and (in the event that there are many candidates for the job) to keep your resume for future reference.

Many people find that it is worthwhile to create two or more versions of their basic resume. You may want an intricately designed resume on high-quality paper to mail or hand out *and* a resume that is designed to be scanned into a computer and saved on a database or an online job site. You can even create a resume in ASCII text to E-mail to prospective employers. For further information, you may wish to refer to the *Guide to Internet Job Searching*, by Frances Roehm and Margaret Dikel, updated and published every other year by VGM Career Books, a division of the McGraw-Hill Companies. This excellent book contains helpful and detailed information about formatting a resume for Internet use. To get you started, in Chapter 3 we have included a list of things to keep in mind when creating electronic resumes.

Although it is usually a good idea to include an objective, in some cases this element is not necessary. The goal of the objective statement is to provide the employer with an idea of where you see yourself going in the field. However, if you are uncertain of the exact nature of the job you seek, including an objective that is too specific could result in your not being considered for a host of perfectly acceptable positions. If you decide not to use an objective heading in your resume, you should definitely incorporate the information that would be conveyed in the objective into your cover letter.

Work Experience

Work experience is arguably the most important element of them all. Unless you are a recent graduate or former homemaker with little or no relevant work experience, your current and former positions will provide the central focus of the resume. You will want this section to be as complete and carefully constructed as possible. By thoroughly examining your work experience, you can get to the heart of your accomplishments and present them in a way that demonstrates and highlights your qualifications.

If you are just entering the workforce, your resume will probably focus on your education, but you should also include information on your work or volunteer experiences. Although you will have less information about work experience than a person who has held multiple positions or is advanced in his or her career, the amount of information is not what is most important in this section. How the information is presented and what it says about you as a worker and a person are what really count.

As you create this section of your resume, remember the need for accuracy. Include all the necessary information about each of your jobs, including your job title, dates of employment, name of your employer, city, state, responsibilities, special projects you handled, and accomplishments. Be sure to list only accomplishments for which you were directly responsible. And don't be alarmed if you haven't participated in or worked on special projects, because this section may not be relevant to certain jobs.

The most common way to list your work experience is in *reverse chronological order*. In other words, start with your most recent job and work your way backward. This way, your prospective employer sees your current (and often most important) position before considering your past employment. Your most recent position, if it's the most important in terms of responsibilities and relevance to the job for which you are applying, should also be the one that includes the most information as compared to your previous positions.

Even if the work itself seems unrelated to your proposed career path, you should list any job or experience that will help sell your talents. If you were promoted or given greater responsibilities or commendations, be sure to mention the fact.

The following worksheet is provided to help you organize your experiences in the working world. It will also serve as an excellent resource to refer to when updating your resume in the future.

WORK EXPERIENCE

Job One:

Job Title _____

Dates _____

Employer _____

City, State _____

Major Duties _____

_____

_____

_____

_____

_____

_____

_____

_____

Special Projects _____

_____

_____

_____

Accomplishments _____

_____

_____

_____

_____

_____

Job Two:

Job Title _____

Dates _____

Employer _____

City, State _____

Major Duties _____

_____

_____

_____

_____

_____

_____

Special Projects _____

_____

_____

_____

Accomplishments _____

_____

_____

_____

_____

_____

_____

_____

Job Three:

Job Title _____

Dates _____

Employer _____

City, State _____

Major Duties _____

_____

_____

_____

_____

_____

_____

_____

Special Projects _____

_____

_____

_____

Accomplishments _____

_____

_____

_____

_____

_____

_____

_____

_____

Job Four:

Job Title _____

Dates _____

Employer _____

City, State _____

Major Duties _____

_____

_____

_____

_____

_____

_____

_____

Special Projects _____

_____

_____

_____

Accomplishments _____

_____

_____

_____

_____

_____

_____

_____

Education

Education is usually the second most important element of a resume. Your educational background is often a deciding factor in an employer's decision to interview you. Highlight your accomplishments in school as much as you did those accomplishments at work. If you are looking for your first professional job, your education or life experience will be your greatest asset because your related work experience will be minimal. In this case, the education section becomes the most important means of selling yourself.

Include in this section all the degrees or certificates you have received; your major or area of concentration; all of the honors you earned; and any relevant activities you participated in, organized, or chaired. Again, list your most recent schooling first. If you have completed graduate-level work, begin with that and work your way back through your undergraduate education. If you have completed college, you generally should not list your high school experience; do so only if you earned special honors, you had a grade point average that was much better than the norm, or this was your highest level of education.

If you have completed a large number of credit hours in a subject that may be relevant to the position you are seeking but did not obtain a degree, you may wish to list the hours or classes you completed. Keep in mind, however, that you may be asked to explain why you did not finish the program. If you are currently in school, list the degree, certificate, or license you expect to obtain and the projected date of completion.

The following worksheet will help you gather the information you need for this section of your resume.

EDUCATION

School One _____

Major or Area of Concentration _____

Degree _____

Dates _____

School Two _____

Major or Area of Concentration _____

Degree _____

Dates _____

Honors

If you include an honors section in your resume, you should highlight any awards, honors, or memberships in honorary societies that you have received. (You may also incorporate this information into your education section.) Often, the honors are academic in nature, but this section also may be used for special achievements in sports, clubs, or other school activities. Always include the name of the organization awarding the honor and the date(s) received. Use the following worksheet to help you gather your information.

HONORS

Honor One _____

Awarding Organization _____

Date(s) _____

Honor Two _____

Awarding Organization _____

Date(s) _____

Honor Three _____

Awarding Organization _____

Date(s) _____

Honor Four _____

Awarding Organization _____

Date(s) _____

Honor Five _____

Awarding Organization _____

Date(s) _____

Activities

Perhaps you have been active in different organizations or clubs; often an employer will look at such involvement as evidence of initiative, dedication, and good social skills. Examples of your ability to take a leading role in a group should be included on a resume, if you can provide them. The activities section of your resume should present neighborhood and community activities, volunteer positions, and so forth. In general, you may want to avoid listing any organization whose name indicates the race, creed, sex, age, marital status, sexual orientation, or nation of origin of its members because this could expose you to discrimination. Use the following worksheet to list the specifics of your activities.

ACTIVITIES

Organization/Activity   _____

Accomplishments   _____

_____

_____

Organization/Activity _____

Accomplishments   _____

_____

_____

Organization/Activity   _____

Accomplishments   _____

_____

_____

As your work experience grows through the years, your school activities and honors will carry less weight and be emphasized less in your resume. Eventually, you will probably list only your degree and any major honors received. As time goes by, your job performance and the experience you've gained become the most important elements in your resume, which should change to reflect this.

Certificates and Licenses

If your chosen career path requires specialized training, you may already have certificates or licenses. You should list these if the job you are seeking requires them and you, of course, have acquired them. If you have applied for a license but have not yet received it, use the phrase "application pending."

License requirements vary by state. If you have moved or are planning to relocate to another state, check with that state's board or licensing agency for all licensing requirements.

Always make sure that all of the information you list is completely accurate. Locate copies of your certificates and licenses, and check the exact date and name of the accrediting agency. Use the following worksheet to organize the necessary information.

CERTIFICATES AND LICENSES

Name of License _____

Licensing Agency _____

Date Issued _____

Name of License _____

Licensing Agency _____

Date Issued _____

Name of License _____

Licensing Agency _____

Date Issued _____

Publications

Some professions strongly encourage or even require that you publish. If you have written, coauthored, or edited any books, articles, professional papers, or works of a similar nature that pertain to your field, you will definitely want to include this element. Remember to list the date of publication and the publisher's name, and specify whether you were the sole author or a coauthor. Book, magazine, or journal titles are generally italicized, while the titles of articles within a larger publication appear in quotes. (Check with your reference librarian for more about the appropriate way to present this information.) For scientific or research papers, you will need to give the date, place, and audience to whom the paper was presented.

Use the following worksheet to help you gather the necessary information about your publications.

PUBLICATIONS

Title and Type (Note, Article, etc.) _____

Title of Publication (Journal, Book, etc.) _____

Publisher _____

Date Published _____

Title and Type (Note, Article, etc.) _____

Title of Publication (Journal, Book, etc.) _____

Publisher _____

Date Published _____

Title and Type (Note, Article, etc.) _____

Title of Publication (Journal, Book, etc.) _____

Publisher _____

Date Published _____

Professional Memberships

Another potential element in your resume is a section listing professional memberships. Use this section to describe your involvement in professional associations, unions, and similar organizations. It is to your advantage to list any professional memberships that pertain to the job you are seeking. Many employers see your membership as representative of your desire to stay up-to-date and connected in your field. Include the dates of your involvement and whether you took part in any special activities or held any offices within the organization. Use the following worksheet to organize your information.

PROFESSIONAL MEMBERSHIPS

Name of Organization _____

Office(s) Held_____

Activities _____

Dates _____

Name of Organization _____

Office(s) Held_____

Activities _____

Dates _____

Name of Organization _____

Office(s) Held_____

Activities _____

Dates _____

Name of Organization _____

Office(s) Held_____

Activities _____

Dates _____

Special Skills

The special skills section of your resume is the place to mention any special abilities you have that relate to the job you are seeking. You can use this element to present certain talents or experiences that are not necessarily a part of your education or work experience. Common examples include fluency in a foreign language, extensive travel abroad, or knowledge of a particular computer application. "Special skills" can encompass a wide range of talents, and this section can be used creatively. However, for each skill you list, you should be able to describe how it would be a direct asset in the type of work you're seeking because employers may ask just that in an interview. If you can't think of a way to do this, it may be extraneous information.

Personal Information

Some people include personal information on their resumes. This is generally not recommended, but you might wish to include it if you think that something in your personal life, such as a hobby or talent, has some bearing on the position you are seeking. This type of information is often referred to at the beginning of an interview, when it may be used as an icebreaker. Of course, personal information regarding your age, marital status, race, religion, or sexual orientation should never appear on your resume as personal information. It should be given only in the context of memberships and activities, and only when doing so would not expose you to discrimination.

References

References are not usually given on the resume itself, but a prospective employer needs to know that you have references who may be contacted if necessary. All you need to include is a single sentence at the end of the resume: "References are available upon request," or even simply, "References available." Have a reference list ready—your interviewer may ask to see it! Contact each person on the list ahead of time to see whether it is all right for you to use him or her as a reference. This way, the person has a chance to think about what to say *before* the call occurs. This helps ensure that you will obtain the best reference possible.

Chapter 2

Writing Your Resume

Now that you have gathered the information for each section of your resume, it's time to write it out in a way that will get the attention of the reviewer—hopefully, your future employer! The language you use in your resume will affect its success, so you must be careful and conscientious. Translate the facts you have gathered into the active, precise language of resume writing. You will be aiming for a resume that keeps the reader's interest and highlights your accomplishments in a concise and effective way.

Resume writing is unlike any other form of writing. Although your seventh-grade composition teacher would not approve, the rules of punctuation and sentence building are often completely ignored. Instead, you should try for a functional, direct writing style that focuses on the use of verbs and other words that imply action on your part. Writing with action words and strong verbs characterizes you to potential employers as an energetic, active person, someone who completes tasks and achieves results from his or her work. Resumes that do not make use of action words can sound passive and stale. These resumes are not effective and do not get the attention of any employer, no matter how qualified the applicant. Choose words that display your strengths and demonstrate your initiative. The following list of commonly used verbs will help you create a strong resume:

administered	assembled
advised	assumed responsibility
analyzed	billed
arranged	built

carried out	inspected
channeled	interviewed
collected	introduced
communicated	invented
compiled	maintained
completed	managed
conducted	met with
contacted	motivated
contracted	negotiated
coordinated	operated
counseled	orchestrated
created	ordered
cut	organized
designed	oversaw
determined	performed
developed	planned
directed	prepared
dispatched	presented
distributed	produced
documented	programmed
edited	published
established	purchased
expanded	recommended
functioned as	recorded
gathered	reduced
handled	referred
hired	represented
implemented	researched
improved	reviewed

saved	supervised
screened	taught
served as	tested
served on	trained
sold	typed
suggested	wrote

Let's look at two examples that differ only in their writing style. The first resume section is ineffective because it does not use action words to accent the applicant's work experiences.

WORK EXPERIENCE
Regional Sales Manager

Manager of sales representatives from seven states. Manager of twelve food chain accounts in the East. In charge of the sales force's planned selling toward specific goals. Supervisor and trainer of new sales representatives. Consulting for customers in the areas of inventory management and quality control.

Special Projects: Coordinator and sponsor of annual food-industry sales seminar.

Accomplishments: Monthly regional volume went up 25 percent during my tenure while, at the same time, a proper sales/cost ratio was maintained. Customer-company relations were improved.

In the following paragraph, we have rewritten the same section using action words. Notice how the tone has changed. It now sounds stronger and more active. This person accomplished goals and really *did* things.

WORK EXPERIENCE
Regional Sales Manager

Managed sales representatives from seven states. Oversaw twelve food chain accounts in the eastern United States. Directed the sales force in planned selling toward specific goals. Supervised and trained new sales representatives. Counseled customers in the areas of inventory management and quality control. Coordinated and sponsored the annual Food Industry Seminar. Increased monthly regional volume by 25 percent and helped to improve customer–company relations during my tenure.

One helpful way to construct the work experience section is to make use of your actual job descriptions—the written duties and expectations your employers had for a person in your current or former position. Job descriptions are rarely written in proper resume language, so you will have to rework them, but they do include much of the information necessary to create this section of your resume. If you have access to job descriptions for your former positions, you can use the details to construct an action-oriented paragraph. Often, your human resources department can provide a job description for your current position.

The following is an example of a typical human resources job description, followed by a rewritten version of the same description employing action words and specific details about the job. Again, pay attention to the style of writing instead of the content, as the details of your own experience will be unique.

WORK EXPERIENCE
Public Administrator I

Responsibilities: Coordinate and direct public services to meet the needs of the nation, state, or community. Analyze problems; work with special committees and public agencies; recommend solutions to governing bodies.

Aptitudes and Skills: Ability to relate to and communicate with people; solve complex problems through analysis; plan, organize, and implement policies and programs. Knowledge of political systems, financial management, personnel administration, program evaluation, and organizational theory.

WORK EXPERIENCE
Public Administrator I

Wrote pamphlets and conducted discussion groups to inform citizens of legislative processes and consumer issues. Organized and supervised 25 interviewers. Trained interviewers in effective communication skills.

After you have written out your resume, you are ready to begin the next important step: assembly and layout.

Chapter 3

Assembly and Layout

A t this point, you've gathered all the necessary information for your resume and rewritten it in language that will impress your potential employers. Your next step is to assemble the sections in a logical order and lay them out on the page neatly and attractively to achieve the desired effect: getting the interview.

Assembly

The order of the elements in a resume makes a difference in its overall effect. Clearly, you would not want to bury your name and address somewhere in the middle of the resume. Nor would you want to lead with a less important section, such as special skills. Put the elements in an order that stresses your most important accomplishments and the things that will be most appealing to your potential employer. For example, if you are new to the workforce, you will want the reviewer to read about your education and life skills before any part-time jobs you may have held for short durations. On the other hand, if you have been gainfully employed for several years and currently hold an important position in your company, you should list your work accomplishments ahead of your educational information, which has become less pertinent with time.

Certain things should always be included in your resume, but others are optional. The following list shows you which are which. You might want to use it as a checklist to be certain that you have included all of the necessary information.

Essential	**Optional**
Name	Cellular Phone Number
Address	Pager Number
Phone Number	E-Mail Address or Website Address
Work Experience	Voice Mail Number
Education	Job Objective
References Phrase	Honors
	Special Skills
	Publications
	Professional Memberships
	Activities
	Certificates and Licenses
	Personal Information
	Graphics
	Photograph

Your choice of optional sections depends on your own background and employment needs. Always use information that will put you in a favorable light—unless it's absolutely essential, avoid anything that will prompt the interviewer to ask questions about your weaknesses or something else that could be unflattering. Make sure your information is accurate and truthful. If your honors are impressive, include them in the resume. If your activities in school demonstrate talents that are necessary for the job you are seeking, allow space for a section on activities. If you are applying for a position that requires ornamental illustration, you may want to include border illustrations or graphics that demonstrate your talents in this area. If you are answering an advertisement for a job that requires certain physical traits, a photo of yourself might be appropriate. A person applying for a job as a computer programmer would *not* include a photo as part of his or her resume. Each resume is unique, just as each person is unique.

Types of Resumes

So far we have focused on the most common type of resume—the *reverse chronological* resume—in which your most recent job is listed first. This is the type of resume usually preferred by those who have to read a large number of resumes, and it is by far the most popular and widely circulated. However, this style of presentation may not be the most effective way to highlight *your* skills and accomplishments.

For example, if you are reentering the workforce after many years or are trying to change career fields, the *functional* resume may work best. This type of resume puts the focus on your achievements instead of the sequence of your work history. In the functional resume, your experience is presented through your general accomplishments and the skills you have developed in your working life.

A functional resume is assembled from the same information you gathered in Chapter 1. The main difference lies in how you organize the information. Essentially, the work experience section is divided in two, with your job duties and accomplishments constituting one section and your employers' names, cities, and states; your positions; and the dates employed making up the other. Place the first section near the top of your resume, just below your job objective (if used), and call it *Accomplishments* or *Achievements*. The second section, containing the bare essentials of your work history, should come after the accomplishments section and can be called *Employment History*, since it is a chronological overview of your former jobs.

The other sections of your resume remain the same. The work experience section is the only one affected in the functional format. By placing the section that focuses on your achievements at the beginning, you draw attention to these achievements. This puts less emphasis on where you worked and when, and more on what you did and what you are capable of doing.

If you are changing careers, the emphasis on skills and achievements is important. The identities of previous employers (who aren't part of your new career field) need to be downplayed. A functional resume can help accomplish this task. If you are reentering the workforce after a long absence, a functional resume is the obvious choice. And if you lack full-time work experience, you will need to draw attention away from this fact and put the focus on your skills and abilities. You may need to highlight your volunteer activities and part-time work. Education may also play a more important role in your resume.

The type of resume that is right for you will depend on your personal circumstances. It may be helpful to create both types and then compare them. Which one presents you in the best light? Examples of both types of resumes are included in this book. Use the sample resumes in Chapter 5 to help you decide on the content, presentation, and look of your own resume.

Resume or Curriculum Vitae?

A curriculum vitae (CV) is a longer, more detailed synopsis of your professional history, which generally runs three or more pages in length. It includes a summary of your educational and academic background as well as teaching and research experience, publications, presentations, awards, honors, affiliations, and other details. Because the purpose of the CV is different from that of the resume, many of the rules we've discussed thus far involving style and length do not apply.

A curriculum vitae is used primarily for admissions applications to graduate or professional schools, independent consulting in a variety of settings, proposals for fellowships or grants, or applications for positions in academia. As with a resume, you may need different versions of a CV for different types of positions. You should only send a CV when one is specifically requested by an employer or institution.

Like a resume, your CV should include your name, contact information, education, skills and experience. In addition to the basics, a CV includes research and teaching experience, publications, grants and fellowships, professional associations and licenses, awards, and other information relevant to the position for which you are applying. You can follow the advice presented thus far to gather and organize your personal information.

Special Tips for Electronic Resumes

Because there are many details to consider in writing a resume that will be posted or transmitted on the Internet, or one that will be scanned into a computer when it is received, we suggest that you refer to the *Guide to Internet Job Searching*, by Frances Roehm and Margaret Dikel, as previously mentioned. However, here are some brief, general guidelines to follow if you expect your resume to be scanned into a computer.

- Use standard fonts in which none of the letters touch.

- Keep in mind that underlining, italics, and fancy scripts may not scan well.

- Use boldface and capitalization to set off elements. Again, make sure letters don't touch. Leave at least a quarter inch between lines of type.

- Keep information and elements at the left margin. Centering, columns, and even indenting may change when the resume is optically scanned.

- Do not use any lines, boxes, or graphics.

- Place the most important information at the top of the first page. If you use two pages, put "Page 1 of 2" at the bottom of the first page and put your name and "Page 2 of 2" at the top of the second page.

- List each telephone number on its own line in the header.

- Use multiple keywords or synonyms for what you do to make sure your qualifications will be picked up if a prospective employer is searching for them. Use nouns that are keywords for your profession.

- Be descriptive in your titles. For example, don't just use "assistant"; use "legal office assistant."

- Make sure the contrast between print and paper is good. Use a high-quality laser printer and white or very light colored 8½-by-11-inch paper.

- Mail a high-quality laser print or an excellent copy. Do not fold or use staples, as this might interfere with scanning. You may, however, use paper clips.

In addition to creating a resume that works well for scanning, you may want to have a resume that can be E-mailed to reviewers. Because you may not know what word processing application the recipient uses, the best format to use is ASCII text. (ASCII stands for "American Standard Code for Information Exchange.") It allows people with very different software platforms to exchange and understand information. (E-mail operates on this principle.) ASCII is a simple, text-only language, which means you can include only simple text. There can be no use of boldface, italics, or even paragraph indentations.

To create an ASCII resume, just use your normal word processing program; when finished, save it as a "text only" document. You will find this option under the "save" or "save as" command. Here is a list of things to *avoid* when crafting your electronic resume:

- Tabs. Use your space bar. Tabs will not work.

- Any special characters, such as mathematical symbols.

- Word wrap. Use hard returns (the return key) to make line breaks.

- Centering or other formatting. Align everything at the left margin.

- Bold or italic fonts. Everything will be converted to plain text when you save the file as a "text only" document.

Check carefully for any mistakes before you save the document as a text file. Spellcheck and proofread it several times; then ask someone with a keen eye to go over it again for you. Remember: the key is to keep it simple. Any attempt to make this resume pretty or decorative may result in a resume that is confusing and hard to read. After you have saved the document, you can cut and paste it into an E-mail or onto a website.

Layout for a Paper Resume

A great deal of care—and much more formatting—is necessary to achieve an attractive layout for your paper resume. There is no single appropriate layout that applies to every resume, but there are a few basic rules to follow in putting your resume on paper:

- Leave a comfortable margin on the sides, top, and bottom of the page (usually one to one and a half inches).

- Use appropriate spacing between the sections (two to three line spaces are usually adequate).

- Be consistent in the *type* of headings you use for different sections of your resume. For example, if you capitalize the heading EMPLOYMENT HISTORY, don't use initial capitals and underlining for a section of equal importance, such as Education.

- Do not use more than one font in your resume. Stay consistent by choosing a font that is fairly standard and easy to read, and don't change it for different sections. Beware of the tendency to try to make your resume original by choosing fancy type styles; your resume may end up looking unprofessional instead of creative. Unless you are in a very creative and artistic field, you should almost always stick with tried-and-true type styles like Times New Roman and Palatino, which are often used in business writing. In the area of resume styles, conservative is usually the best way to go.

CHRONOLOGICAL RESUME

CHARLES ANDAWA

4783 West Maple • Baltimore, MD 21218
301-555-2983 • Charles.Andawa@xxx.com

Objective

To obtain a position in chemical engineering with an environmental engineering organization.

Recent Experience

1998 - Present
Senior Project Manager, PPD, Inc., Baltimore, MD

- Report to senior vice president of engineering.
- Supervise 32 employees.
- Direct, supervise, administer, and manage projects from inception to start-up, including new chemical process equipment manufacturing.
- Assist sales department in reviewing the system process design, scheduling, engineering, and costs before final proposal is presented to client.
- Conceive, initiate, and develop chemical formations for nontoxic solutions for use in oil recovery and recycling.
- Formulated empirical equations and design criteria for the system, which resulted in increasing company sales seven-fold over the last five years.
- Train project engineers and project managers to design and manage projects.

1994 - 1998
Senior Project Engineer, Moreland Chemical, Annapolis, MD

- Project experience included pulp liquor evaporation system operations, sand reclamation systems, waste wood utilization to manufacture charcoal, sewage sludge oxidation, waste oxidation, and heat recovery.
- Responsible for planning, scheduling, process design, and specifications.

Education

B.S., M.S., Chemical Engineering, 1989
Michigan Technical University - Houghton, MI

FUNCTIONAL RESUME

JUDITH W. SWENSEN

4422 Kennet Avenue   (615) 555-4876
Jubal, Tennessee 37232   Swensen@xxx.com

Summary of Qualifications

Experience in providing comprehensive environmental assistance to mining operations and exploration projects. Maintain an awareness of all federal environmental regulations to assess compliance of subsidiary companies. Conduct detailed environmental audits at mining and terminal locations.

Accomplishments

Solid Waste Disposal
- As disposal methods analyst, charged with determining best disposal method at each subsidiary mine. Methods chosen are site-specific and depend on depth to groundwater, percentage and types of heavy metals present in the coal ash, and column leachate test results.
- Investigated and designed economical solid and hazardous waste disposal options for subsidiary companies.

Mine Drainage Treatment
- Assisted subsidiaries with effective economical methods of controlling acid mine drainage from coal refuse piles and ensuring reclamation success.
- Conducted research with Tennessee State University to determine methods of refuse pretreatment to eliminate further AMD and have successfully installed two systems.

Employment History

Senior Development Specialist, 2003 to present
Smoky Mountain Mining Company, Memphis, TN

Graduate Assistant/Lab Technician, 2000 to 2003
University of Tennessee, Chemical Engineering Department

Education

University of Tennessee
- Ph.D. in Chemical Engineering, 1996
- B.S. in Chemistry and Physics, 1993

- Always try to fit your resume on one page. If you are having trouble with this, you may be trying to say too much. Edit out any repetitive or unnecessary information, and shorten descriptions of earlier jobs where possible. Ask a friend you trust for feedback on what seems unnecessary or unimportant. For example, you may have included too many optional sections. Today, with the prevalence of the personal computer as a tool, there is no excuse for a poorly laid out resume. Experiment with variations until you are pleased with the result.

Remember that a resume is not an autobiography. Too much information will only get in the way. The more compact your resume, the easier it will be to review. If a person who is swamped with resumes looks at yours, catches the main points, and then calls you for an interview to fill in some of the details, your resume has already accomplished its task. A clear and concise resume makes for a happy reader and a good impression.

There are times when, despite extensive editing, the resume simply cannot fit on one page. In this case, the resume should be laid out on two pages in such a way that neither clarity nor appearance is compromised. Each page of a two-page resume should be marked clearly: the first should indicate "Page 1 of 2," and the second should include your name and the page number, for example, "Julia Ramirez—Page 2 of 2." The pages should then be stapled together. You may use a smaller font (in the same font as the body of your resume) for the page numbers. Place them at the bottom of page one and the top of page two. Again, spend the time now to experiment with the layout until you find one that looks good to you.

Always show your final layout to other people and ask them what they like or dislike about it, and what impresses them most when they read your resume. Make sure that their responses are the same as what you want to elicit from your prospective employer. If they aren't the same, you should continue to make changes until the necessary information is emphasized.

Proofreading

After you have finished typing the master copy of your resume and before you have it copied or printed, thoroughly check it for typing and spelling errors. Do not place all your trust in your computer's spellcheck function. Use an old editing trick and read the whole resume backward—start at the end and read it right to left and bottom to top. This can help you see the small errors or inconsistencies that are easy to overlook. Take time to do it right because a single error on a document this important can cause the reader to judge your attention to detail in a harsh light.

Have several people look at the finished resume just in case you've missed an error. Don't try to take a shortcut; not having an unbiased set of eyes examine your resume now could mean embarrassment later. Even experienced editors can easily overlook their own errors. Be thorough and conscientious with your proofreading so your first impression is a perfect one.

We have included the following rules of capitalization and punctuation to assist you in the final stage of creating your resume. Remember that resumes often require use of a shorthand style of writing that may include sentences without periods and other stylistic choices that break the standard rules of grammar. Be consistent in each section and throughout the whole resume with your choices.

RULES OF CAPITALIZATION

- Capitalize proper nouns, such as names of schools, colleges, and universities; names of companies; and brand names of products.

- Capitalize major words in the names and titles of books, tests, and articles that appear in the body of your resume.

- Capitalize words in major section headings of your resume.

- Do not capitalize words just because they seem important.

- When in doubt, consult a style manual such as *Words into Type* (Prentice Hall) or *The Chicago Manual of Style* (The University of Chicago Press). Your local library can help you locate these and other reference books. Many computer programs also have grammar help sections.

RULES OF PUNCTUATION

- Use commas to separate words in a series.

- Use a semicolon to separate series of words that already include commas within the series. (For an example, see the first rule of capitalization.)

- Use a semicolon to separate independent clauses that are not joined by a conjunction.

- Use a period to end a sentence.

- Use a colon to show that examples or details follow that will expand or amplify the preceding phrase.

- Avoid the use of dashes.

- Avoid the use of brackets.

- If you use any punctuation in an unusual way in your resume, be consistent in its use.

- Whenever you are uncertain, consult a style manual.

Putting Your Resume in Print

You will need to buy high-quality paper for your printer before you print your finished resume. Regular office paper is not good enough for resumes; the reviewer will probably think it looks flimsy and cheap. Go to an office supply store or copy shop and select a high-quality bond paper that will make a good first impression. Select colors like white, off-white, or possibly a light gray. In some industries, a pastel may be acceptable, but be sure the color and feel of the paper makes a subtle, positive statement about you. Nothing in the choice of paper should be loud or unprofessional.

If your computer printer does not reproduce your resume properly and produces smudged or stuttered type, either ask to borrow a friend's or take your disk (or a clean original) to a printer or copy shop for high-quality copying. If you anticipate needing a large number of copies, taking your resume to a copy shop or a printer is probably the best choice.

Hold a sheet of your unprinted bond paper up to the light. If it has a watermark, you will want to point this out to the person helping you with copies; the printing should be done so that the reader can read the print and see the watermark the right way up. Check each copy for smudges or streaks. This is the time to be a perfectionist—the results of your careful preparation will be well worth it.

Chapter 4

The Cover Letter

Once your resume has been assembled, laid out, and printed to your satisfaction, the next and final step before distribution is to write your cover letter. Though there may be instances where you deliver your resume in person, you will usually send it through the mail or online. Resumes sent through the mail always need an accompanying letter that briefly introduces you and your resume. The purpose of the cover letter is to get a potential employer to read your resume, just as the purpose of the resume is to get that same potential employer to call you for an interview.

Like your resume, your cover letter should be clean, neat, and direct. A cover letter usually includes the following information:

1. Your name and address (unless it already appears on your personal letterhead) and your phone number(s); see item 7.

2. The date.

3. The name and address of the person and company to whom you are sending your resume.

4. The salutation ("Dear Mr." or "Dear Ms." followed by the person's last name, or "To Whom It May Concern" if you are answering a blind ad).

5. An opening paragraph explaining why you are writing (for example, in response to an ad, as a follow-up to a previous meeting, at the suggestion of someone you both know) and indicating that you are interested in whatever job is being offered.

6. One or more paragraphs that tell why you want to work for the company and what qualifications and experiences you can bring to the position. This is a good place to mention some detail about

that particular company that makes you want to work for them; this shows that you have done some research before applying.

7. A final paragraph that closes the letter and invites the reviewer to contact you for an interview. This can be a good place to tell the potential employer which method would be best to use when contacting you. Be sure to give the correct phone number and a good time to reach you, if that is important. You may mention here that your references are available upon request.

8. The closing ("Sincerely" or "Yours truly") followed by your signature in a dark ink, with your name typed under it.

Your cover letter should include all of this information and be no longer than one page in length. The language used should be polite, businesslike, and to the point. Don't attempt to tell your life story in the cover letter; a long and cluttered letter will serve only to annoy the reader. Remember that you need to mention only a few of your accomplishments and skills in the cover letter. The rest of your information is available in your resume. If your cover letter is a success, your resume will be read and all pertinent information reviewed by your prospective employer.

Producing the Cover Letter

Cover letters should always be individualized because they are always written to specific individuals and companies. Never use a form letter for your cover letter or copy it as you would a resume. Each cover letter should be unique, and as personal and lively as possible. (Of course, once you have written and rewritten your first cover letter until you are satisfied with it, you can certainly use similar wording in subsequent letters. You may want to save a template on your computer for future reference.) Keep a hard copy of each cover letter so you know exactly what you wrote in each one.

There are sample cover letters in Chapter 6. Use them as models or for ideas of how to assemble and lay out your own cover letters. Remember that every letter is unique and depends on the particular circumstances of the individual writing it and the job for which he or she is applying.

After you have written your cover letter, proofread it as thoroughly as you did your resume. Again, spelling or punctuation errors are a sure sign of carelessness, and you don't want that to be a part of your first impression on a prospective employer. This is no time to trust your spellcheck function. Even after going through a spelling and grammar check, your cover letter should be carefully proofread by at least one other person.

Print the cover letter on the same quality bond paper you used for your resume. Remember to sign it, using a good dark-ink pen. Handle the letter and resume carefully to avoid smudging or wrinkling, and mail them together in an appropriately sized envelope. Many stores sell matching envelopes to coordinate with your choice of bond paper.

Keep an accurate record of all resumes you send out and the results of each mailing. This record can be kept on your computer, in a calendar or notebook, or on file cards. Knowing when a resume is likely to have been received will keep you on track as you make follow-up phone calls.

About a week after mailing resumes and cover letters to potential employers, contact them by telephone. Confirm that your resume arrived and ask whether an interview might be possible. Be sure to record the name of the person you spoke to and any other information you gleaned from the conversation. It is wise to treat the person answering the phone with a great deal of respect; sometimes the assistant or receptionist has the ear of the person doing the hiring.

You should make a great impression with the strong, straightforward resume and personalized cover letter you have just created. We wish you every success in securing the career of your dreams!

Chapter 5

Sample Resumes

This chapter contains dozens of sample resumes for people pursuing a wide variety of jobs and careers.

There are many different styles of resumes in terms of graphic layout and presentation of information. These samples represent people with varying amounts of education and experience. Use them as models for your own resume. Choose one resume or borrow elements from several different resumes to help you design your own.

RICHARD J. STEWART
34 King Crossing • Indianapolis, IN 46227
Richard.Stewart@xxx.com • (317) 555-7654

CAREER OBJECTIVE
Desire a position in non-game animal research.

EDUCATION
B.S. in Biology, Minor in Business
Ball State University, Muncie, IN
May 2002

EXPERIENCE
Summers 2000 & 2001
Student Conservation Volunteer and Assistant Biologist
Bureau of Land Management
Indianapolis, IN

STUDENT CONSERVATION VOLUNTEER
Stream Management
Timber Management
Bat Study
• Seventy-five percent of activity was spent in remote areas with minimal supervision.
• Extensive use of topographical maps and aerial photographs.

ASSISTANT BIOLOGIST
• Firth Taxonomy, Electrofishing, Seining
• Statistical Experience: I.J.W.B., M.I.W.B., I.B.I., S.A.S. Computer System
• Conducted Education Tours of Wetlands

References available upon request

MARK LESLIE GISLER

1422 Douglas Drive
Mitchell, IN 47446
(317) 555-2314
MLGisler@xxx.com

EDUCATION

Purdue University, Expected graduation date: June 2004
B.S. in Computer Systems Engineering
M.S. in Engineering-Economic Systems.

Coursework completed by graduation will include 30 quarter-hours of electrical engineering courses, 47 quarter-hours of computer science courses, 27 quarter-hours of engineering-economic systems courses, and 26 quarter-hours of related science and mathematics courses.

Undergraduate coursework includes digital design, VLSI design, computer architecture, concurrent programming, operating systems, and databases.

Graduate coursework includes dynamic systems, decision analysis, optimization, probability theory, and several courses about expert systems and computer networks. Honors project involves studying the use of computer networks at Purdue University to allow students to vote on various issues from their dorm rooms, and the effect of such technology on voter participation and awareness.

WORK EXPERIENCE

June 2002-September 2002
Computer Programmer, Lumbermen's Underwriting Alliance
Was responsible for designing and implementing software to supplement the SOLID (Simple On-Line Interface to Databases) project. Wrote two SOLID servers, one in C, the other in Pascal, to allow both HP 3000 minicomputers and HP9000 workstations to accept multiple connections from remote SOLID clients and service clients' requests by dynamically accessing ALLBASE databases.

September 2000-June 2002
Elections Commissioner, Tufts University
Responsibilities included appointing members of the Elections Commission, implementing and supervising all student government elections at the university.

June 1999-September 2000
Computer Programmer, Boeing Corporation
Created software to convert text documents between several word processing formats. Also created an elementary knowledge-base system using CLIPS on the Macintosh to perform analysis of an installation's security needs and deficiencies.

REFERENCES UPON REQUEST

DIANE BRONOWSKI
3355 Brookshire Parkway • Chicago, IL 60636
(312) 555-4948 • D.Bronowski@xxx.com

OBJECTIVE: I hope to utilize my communication, problem-solving, and decision-making skills in a challenging programmer/analyst position with opportunities for advancement.

EDUCATION: ITT Technical Institute, Associate Degree in Computer Programming

EXPERIENCE: Programmer Technician, SERVICE SOFTWARE INC.
May 2000 to Present
- Develop and maintain applications for various departments, create screen formats for program accessing.
- Train end users in basic procedures, on-site and at manufacturing sites out of state.

Systems Analyst, NEW WORLD PACKAGING
June 1997 to May 2000
- Responsible for specifications writing, modifying existing programs as necessary, and designing and coding new programs.
- Performed structural procedure testing, organized data and program modifications, recompiling and rebinding, testing, and debugging.

**TECHNICAL
SKILLS:**
Languages
- COBOL, COBOL II, FORTRAN, SQL, BAL, BASIC

Systems
- MVS/JCL, MVS/ESA, EASYTRIEVE, DOS/VS/VSE, MS DOS

Software
- VSAM, IBM, DB, CICS, DB2, QUICKEN, EASE

REFERENCES AVAILABLE

Regina B. Hernandez

19087 Shadowcrest Ave.
Louisville, CO 80027
(303) 555-9876
R.Hernandez@xxx.com

Education:

B.A. in Chemistry
University of Colorado, 1998

M.S. in Material Science and Engineering
University of Colorado, 2001

Candidate for Ph.D. in Material Science and
Engineering
University of Colorado, date expected: June 2003

Experience:

Summer 2000
Assistant Physicist
General Aircraft Corporation, Boulder, CO

Summer 1999
Graduate Research Assistant
Department of Material Science and Engineering
University of Colorado

Research Topic: Stress Corrosion Cracking in
Aircalory Nuclear Fuel Cladding: Accelerated
SCC Testing of Cladding, Chemical Compatibility

Summer 1998
Undergraduate Research Project
Department of Chemical Engineering
University of Colorado

Research Topic: Design of equipment to be used
to study the coating of a rotating surface with
a viscous fluid.

References Available

ALLEN FISHER

88 Waverly Road • Huntington, IN 46872 • (317) 555-9876
Allen.Fisher@xxx.com

OBJECTIVE

A position in the architectural/engineering/interiors field with emphasis on the CADD environment.

EXPERIENCE

April 2000 - Present
Tad Technical Services (Dow Chemical Company) as a CADD Drafter.
• Working on a team revising drawings to "as built" status.
• Working with Digital VAX station 3100 computer running Autotrol Release 8.2 software on VAXNMS V5.3-1 operating system.

January 2000 - April 2000
Manpower Technical Services (DBC Architects, Inc.) as a CADD Drafter.
• Duties included drafting up revision on floor plans, reflected ceiling plans, schedules, and details on various projects.
• Worked with a Compaq 386 computer running Autocad Release 10 software.

July 1999 - January 2000
SAL, Inc. as a CADD Drafter.
• Duties included space planning, details, and product design of various fast-food restaurants.
• Worked with a Compaq 386 (clone) computer running Cadmaza software.
• Exposure to UNIX on Sun Sparcstation.

September 1998 - June 1999
Boeing Products, Inc. as a CADD Drafter (Autocad)

October 1997 - August 1998
West's Architects, Inc. as a CADD Drafter (Autocad)

EDUCATION
- M.S., Operations Research - Syracuse University, NY
- M.Sc., Statistics - Stanford University, CA
- B.Sc., Mathematics - Duke University, NC

SKILLS
- BASIC
- COBOL
- FORTRAN
- Pascal
- Excel
- Lotus 1-2-3

MEMBERSHIPS
- Operations Research Society of America
- Society for Industrial and Applied Mathematics
- American Association of Computer Professionals

REFERENCES
A detailed list of professional references will be provided on request.

Marie Farrell

Tulane University, 568 Cowell Lane

New Orleans, LA 70118

E-mail: Marie.Farrell@xxx.com

Phone: (504) 555-9876

OBJECTIVE   A challenging project involving software programming.

EDUCATION   Pursuing a B.S. in Computer Systems Engineering.
Tulane University, New Orleans, LA
Anticipated date of graduation: June 2004

Coursework includes Physics, Electronics, Computer Science, Mechanics, Thermodynamics, and Humanities

PROJECTS   March 2004
<u>dbase 3t</u>
Developed a billing system for a small TV repair business.

June 2003
<u>Animation Project</u>
Developed an animation package on the Macintosh.

May 2003
<u>Parallel Programming</u>
Developed some concurrent programs using C++.

December 2003
<u>Logic Design Projects</u>
Designed different digital projects like serial ALU, serial multiplier, associative memories, etc., using PALs and XXVII.

June 2002
<u>Coordinator for Electronics Exhibition</u>
University of Engineering and Technology, Indianapolis, IN
Made arrangements for the installation and security of the projects. Provided necessary information regarding the exhibits to the visitors.

REFERENCES   Available

RUSSELL E. WHITE

1510 East 46th Street • Indianapolis, IN 46220
Russell.White@xxx.com • (317) 555-2118

JOB OBJECTIVE

To obtain a position that would utilize my education in geology.

EDUCATION

- B.A. in Geology from Purdue University - June 2000
- M.S. in Computer Science from Indiana University - expected in June 2002

WORK EXPERIENCE

July 1998 to Present
Holiday Inn in Lafayette, IN
Responsible for the nightly audit.

Summer 2001
Purdue University, Rock Springs, WY
Graduate Assistant to Dr. Peter Strong, Geology Professor

EQUIPMENT EXPERIENCE

- Alidade
- Polarizing microscope

COMPUTER KNOWLEDGE

C, LISP, PASCAL, FORTRAN, PROLOG, SMALLTALK, BASIC

ADDITIONAL SKILLS

- Fluent in German
- Licensed pilot

REFERENCES AVAILABLE

MARTHA K. BAERS

22 Verra Drive ■ Iowa City, Iowa 52242
MKBaers@xxx.com ■ (319) 555-3546

■ Objective

An entry-level position in construction management that will allow me to utilize my technical, organizational, and interpersonal skills to assist with project control tanks.

■ Education

Buena Vista College, Storm Lake, Iowa
Department of Civil Engineering
Master of Science Degree Candidate, May 2002
Construction Engineering and Management

University of Iowa, Iowa City, Iowa
School of Civil and Environmental Engineering
Bachelor of Science Degree, May 2000

■ Coursework

Construction Project Organization and Control
Construction Management
Legal Aspects of the Construction Process
Decision Analysis in Construction
Risk Analysis and Management
Engineering Economics and Management
Building Construction and Earthwork
Heavy Construction and Earthwork
Concrete Materials and Construction
Civil Engineering Materials
Structural Engineering
Geotechnical Engineering
Highway Engineering

■ *Experience*

Research Assistant, January 2001 - Present
Buena Vista College
Storm Lake, Iowa

- Researched several design- and construction-related areas of bituminous materials as part of the Strategic Highway Research Program sponsored by the Federal Highway Administration.
- Published an industrywide report covering the entire scope of the research.

Staff Engineer, May 1999 - August 2000
Schnabel Engineering Associates
Denver, Colorado

- Assisted in the preparation of a complete operation and maintenance manual for a leachate treatment plant and provided support in the compilation and review of all operation- and maintenance-related submittals from the general contractor and all subcontractors.

■ *Achievements*

Engineer-in-Training (EIT) Certification
Dean's List, College of Engineering, Buena Vista College
Dean's List, College of Engineering, University of Iowa

■ *Skills*

Computer Languages: FORTRAN, Pascal, BASIC

Software: Lotus 1-2-3, SuperCalc, Excel, SAS, AutoCAD, Word, MacWrite/WriteNow Harvard Graphics

Fluency in German

■ *Memberships*

Student Member, American Society of Civil Engineers
Student Member, American Concrete Institute

■ *References*

Available upon request

Martin Garcia

2310 Eden Forest Drive
Carmel, IN 46032
Martin.Garcia@xxx.com
(317) 555-9876

Career Interests

Position as an analytical chemist in a research and development or process environment.

Qualifications

Over fifteen years' experience as an analytical chemist with manufacturer of bulk and specialty organic chemicals. Direct responsibility for ensuring quality of a multimillion-dollar production facility. Extensive knowledge and experience in instrumental methods with strong focus on chromatography. Experience with GC/Mass Spectrometry. Systems manager of Perkin Elmer LIMS system.

Work Experience

ABC Industries, Inc., Noblesville, IN (January 2000 - Present)
Core Responsibilities:
 • *Management of quality control and analytical ABC laboratory*
 • *Analytical research and development*
 • *Customer support*
 • *Statistical quality control*
 • *Systems management of laboratory automation system*
Supervisor, Production Analytical Laboratory (May 2001 - Present)
Job Duties:
 • *Analytical equipment maintenance*
 • *Analytical research and development*
 • *Specification and selection of analytical equipment*
 • *Systems management of laboratory automation system*
Senior Analytical Chemist (January 2000 - May 2001)
Job Duties:
 • *Analytical research and development for ten production units*
 • *Troubleshooting process and research problems*
 • *Management of equipment and analytical methodology*
 • *Training*

Work Experience (cont.)

ChemCo Industries, Indianapolis, IN
<u>Analytical Chemist (July 1995 - January 2000)</u>
Job Duties:
- *Routine and nonroutine analysis using a variety of instrumental and classical techniques.*

Education

B.S., Chemistry, 1995
Butler University, Indianapolis, IN

Currently pursuing Master's in Chemistry at Purdue University

Graduate Courses Completed:
- *Chromatographic Methods*
- *Advanced Organic Chemistry*
- *Biochemistry*
- *Heterocyclic Chemistry*
- *Numerical Methods*
- *Advanced Analytical Chemistry*

Additional Training

Microprocessor and Minicomputers (ACS)
Capillary Gas Chromatography (ACS)
Experimental Design and Optimization Routines (DuPont)
Analytical Laboratory Management (McGraw-Hill)

References Available

Mark L. Travers

28 Octabia Terrace
Cincinnati, Ohio 45201
513-555-4063

Goals and Interests

The opportunity to pursue a career in the computer science field as a
programmer/analyst with a quality organization.

Education

Bachelor of Arts Degree, August 2000
Business major with an emphasis on Computer Science, GPA: 3.5/4.0
Western State College, Gunnison, Colorado

Associate of Arts Degree, May 1998
Northeastern Junior College, Sterling, Colorado

Employment

Analyst/User Consultant
IUPUI, Indianapolis, Indiana
Programming on VAX.

Programmer and System Analyst
Western State College, Gunnison, Colorado

Wrote programs in academic years of 1996 - 1997 and 1997 - 1998.
Most programs involved working with POISE.

Computer Skills

Knowledge of C and Pascal programming languages

Familiar with UNIX, VMS, AOS/VS, and MS-DOS operating systems

Proficient in WordPerfect, Ventura Publisher, and Hotshot Graphics

ALLEGHENY COLLEGE
CAREER PLACEMENT CENTER
MEADVILLE, PENNSYLVANIA 16335

NAME: Allen Day
ADDRESS: 88 State Street, Carmel, IN 46032
E-MAIL: Allen.Day68@xxx.com
PHONE: (317) 555-3175

OBJECTIVE To obtain a position in information systems, software
design/development, or related area utilizing computer
programming language skills.

EDUCATION Allegheny College, Meadville, PA
B.S., Computer Science
Graduation Date: June 2004

EXPERIENCE
Summer 2003: City of Reading, Pennsylvania
Management Information Systems Intern
Duties included personal computer assembly and setup
(hardware and software installation) as well as system
troubleshooting. Involved significant user interaction and
operating system knowledge. Worked on IBM PC ATs
and XTs, HP Bectra PCs using MS DOS 3.3

Summer 2002: Indiana University, Indianapolis, IN
Student Programmer
Developed application that aids in vision/perception
research by performing linear transformations to bitmap
images. Consultant to supervisor.

Summer 2001: Indiana University, Indianapolis, IN
Research Programmer
Developed an IBM application for desktop security and
screen-saver.

SKILL SUMMARY
Computer: C, Pascal, Lisp. Also familiar with Ada, Smalltalk, Prolog,
68000 Assembly Language. Procedural, Functional Object-
oriented programming. LightSpeed, MDS environments.

REFERENCES Available on Request

EDWARD J. FISHER

1456 Burlington Ave.   Cincinnati, Ohio 45642   Edward.Fisher@xxx.com   (513) 555-8976

CAREER OBJECTIVE

A cost-effective performer with a proven record of accomplishment, my career objective is to utilize my management, marketing, and computer service experience to make an immediate contribution as a member of a professional management team.

OPERATING SYSTEMS EXPERTISE

- MVSIXA
- CICS
- Vtam
- CA/I
- CA/7
- NCP
- SURPRA
- VPS
- ACF2
- Omegamon

HARDWARE

- IBM 309X and 308X
- IBM 4331
- StorageTek 4400 ACS

EDUCATION

Computer Science Degree
Rose-Hulman Institute of Technology
Terre Haute, Indiana

Master's in Business
University of Notre Dame
South Bend, Indiana

CAREER SUMMARY

OPERATIONS MANAGER, 1999 - Present
Genair Corporation - Cincinnati, OH
Achievements:
- Directed implementation of new data center, hired and trained operations and network personnel. Brought on line ten months ahead of schedule.
- Reduced printing costs by 50 percent resulting in an annual savings of $1.5M by managing a project team through the analysis, design, development, and implementation of new printing systems and procedures.
- Installed corporate telecommunication systems including PBXs, key systems, and national contract with a major carrier resulting in a savings of over $1M.
- Planned and monitored annual operating budget, supervising technical staff consisting of 25 supervisors, analysts, operators, and remote schedulers.
- Coordinated hardware acquisitions and lease negotiations for all nationwide corporate facilities.
- Selected for Executive Loan Program for United Way and Chamber of Commerce.

OPERATIONS MANAGER, 1990 to 1999
Information Services Agency - Dayton, OH
Achievements:
- Initiated automated problem-resolution system resulting in reduction of recurring problems and elimination of tedious manual system.
- Developed position titles and pay scales, which resulted in identifiable career paths for operations personnel.

PROFESSIONAL TRAINING
- Managing Data Processing, IBM
- Data Processing Operations Management, IBM
- Turning Telephone Costs into Profits, University of Notre Dame

PROFESSIONAL AFFILIATIONS
- ITUA - Indiana Telecommunications User Association
- AFCOM - Association for Computer Operations Managers

JOSEPH R. RADER
7128 Woodbrook Place N.E. • Westfield, Indiana 46227
(812) 555-9103

GOALS
The opportunity to work for a quality organization that will allow me to pursue a career in the computer science field as a programmer/analyst.

EDUCATION
Texas Tech University, Lubbock, Texas
Bachelor of Arts Degree, August 1999
Major: Business
Emphasis: Computer Science
GPA: 3.2/4.0

Texas Southern University, Houston, Texas
Associate of Arts Degree, May 1997

EMPLOYMENT
Analyst/User Consultant, September 1999 to Present
Marion College - Indianapolis, Indiana
Programming on VAX.

Student Programmer, January 1999 to August 1999
Texas Tech University, Lubbock, Texas
Wrote programs in BASIC on the VAX 8530.
Most programs involved working with POISE.

Tutor, September 1997 to December 1998
Texas Southern University, Houston, Texas
Tutored students in computer programming classes.

ACCOMPLISHMENTS
Outstanding Student in Computer Science Award
Math/Science Department, Texas Tech University

Computer Science Internship

QUALIFICATIONS
Programming languages: COBOL, Pascal, C, BASIC
(VAX and Apple), FORTRAN, DBASE 111+

Operating systems: VMS, DOS, Apple, Macintosh, UNIX

17 credit hours in upper division computer sciences courses

REFERENCES AVAILABLE

darnell grant

**800 York Ave. South
Minneapolis, MN 55410
(612) 555-7908
D.Grant@xxx.com**

education

B.S. Mechanical Engineering Tech
Rose-Hulman Institute of Technology, 2000
(GPA: 5.75/6.00 on a 6.0 scale)

employment

July 2000 to present TECHNASTAR DESIGN DEVELOPMENT
Development and Design Engineer (7/00 to 1/01)

Responsible for the design and applications of product components
for automotive plastic body panels. This included recommending
design changes and testing products as to their reliability and
durability.

Project Engineer (1/01 to present)

As a project engineer I was involved in manufacturing procedures,
processing improvements, and troubleshooting production problems
for tooling. I managed maintenance activities and vendor contracts
for production tooling.

technical skills

Computer-AutoCAD, BASIC, Lotus, VP Expert

affiliations

Member of Society of Automotive Engineers
Member of Society of Plastics Engineers

NATHAN BUELT

412 S. First Street
Carmel, IN 46032
Nate.Buelt@xxx.com
(317) 555-8976

CAREER OBJECTIVE

To apply excavation experience and develop environmental engineering knowledge with a successful engineering firm.

EDUCATION

Wabash College
B.S. Civil Engineering
Expected completion date: June 2003

TRAINING

Technical electives taken during education:

Environmental Engineering	Urban Planning & Design
Engineering Hydrology	Hydraulic Engineering
Road & Pavement Design	Conservation
Soil Analysis & Composition	Computer Aided Design (CAD)

EXPERIENCE

Construction worker, Summers: 1996 to 2001
Ely Brothers Construction, South Bend, IN

➤ Operated heavy equipment doing excavation work
➤ Installed storm sewer, sanitary sewer, and waterline pipe
➤ Helped set intermediate working stakes
➤ Read blueprints and subdivision layouts
➤ Retention pond construction

ACTIVITIES

➤ Member of American Society of Civil Engineers
➤ Member and secretary of Phi Kappa Theta social fraternity

Mary Ellen White

<u>School Address</u>
Duke University
P.O. Box 55
Durham, North Carolina 27706
(919) 555-9087

<u>Home Address</u>
345 Prospect Road
Cleveland, OH 44136
Mary.White@xxx.com
(419) 555-9087

CAREER OBJECTIVE

A position in civil engineering with an emphasis on design and analysis of structures.

EDUCATION

Duke University
Durham, North Carolina
Graduation Date: May 2001
School of Civil Engineering

Duke University
Durham, North Carolina
Associate of Science Degree
Graduation Date: May 1999

WORK EXPERIENCE

United Technologies Automotive, Inc.
Edinburgh, IN 46124
May to September 1999
• Calculated construction quantities
• Studied blueprints
• Calculated cut and fill on computer

Duke University Study Skills Lab
Durham, North Carolina
August 1998 to May 1999
• Mathematics, physics, and engineering tutor

HONORS AND ACTIVITIES

• Society of Women Engineers
• Phi Sigma Rho Engineering Sorority
• American Society of Civil Engineers

REFERENCES AVAILABLE

JEFFERY LIEN

1908 Greenbay Avenue • Honolulu, HI 96882
Jeff.Lien@xxx.com • (808) 555-9111

EDUCATION

B.S. Mechanical Engineering Technology
Purdue University, Lafayette, IN
1990

EXPERIENCE

1990 - present
Ferguson Steel, Indianapolis, IN

Manager EGL LS Electro Galvanizing Company
Responsible for day-to-day operations.
- Maintain interaction between company and customers.
- Establish company and personal goals for all employees, and manage the execution of said goals.

Mechanical Engineer Maintenance
- Acted as consultant to design engineers on maintenance matters.
- Interacted with Sumitomo (Partner) LTV Engineering, RT Patterson, Dravo, and other engineering firms.

General Foreman General Maintenance and Service
- Supervised 500 plus employees in crafts and trades shops.

Supervisor of Planning Eastern Division
- Supervised engineers and financial analyst in the planning and justification of maintenance projects.
- Served on the contracting out committee.

ADDITIONAL INFORMATION

Fluent in Spanish
Working knowledge of German, French, and Italian

REFERENCES

Available

John Broad

1544 Carmel Drive
Carmel, IN 46032
J.Broad@xxx.com
(317) 555-9786

Objective

Senior Mechanical Engineering position with major corporation engaged in advanced aircraft research and development.

Experience

Technical and manufacturing problem-solving experience for a major aerospace firm. Test and evaluation training.

5/91 - Present   Flight Corporation, Indianapolis, IN

Flight Test Engineer
Structural Loads and Dynamics
- Supervised a test program to demonstrate to the Air Force the ability of advanced fighter-bomber aircraft to perform on an aircraft carrier with no adverse effects to the structure. Applied experience to advise flight and Air Force test pilots and assist flight engineers with data analysis in the development of graphite fiber composite wings.
- Implemented extensive research and data analysis during the development of forward-swept wing aircraft including envelope expansion and thermal properties.

Manufacturing Engineer
- Utilized CAD/CAM equipment to create numerical controlled programs to fabricate detail aircraft parts. Developed operation procedures to manufacture aircraft details and wing, fuselage, and tail assemblies using high-technology manufacturing processes.
- Successfully implemented laser and optical technology for the construction of aircraft tooling jigs and fixtures.

Education

Iowa State University of Science and Technology
B.S. Mechanical Engineering, 1991

Iowa Technical College
A.A.A. Automotive Technology, 1989

References

Furnished upon request.

MICHAEL E. DAY

• 567 Sherwood Drive • Hawthorne, New York 10532 •
• 914-555-8976 • Michael.Day@xxx.com •

• OBJECTIVE

Managerial or technical position in Data Processing Operations, Data Communications, or Engineering areas.

• SUMMARY

Multifaceted technical manager with ten years' experience in Engineering, Operations, and Data Communications. Major strengths: design and implementation of start-up operation and project team management.

• EXPERIENCE

Automatic Digital Corporation, 1991 - Present
• Responsibilities are to design and implement the start-up operation and project team management.

Director of Data Communication, 1996 - Present
• Manage and control daily operations of millions of real-time financial services data networks supporting international and domestic clients.
• Managed, planned, and executed entire relocation of international data communication network to a new financial processing center in Bridgeport, Connecticut.
• Supervised initial implementation of a TI data communications network to support financial services group.

Director of Engineering/Operations, 1994 - 1996
• Directed and controlled daily operations of financial service processing center along with engineering and repair operations. Developed and administered million-dollar budget. Managed staff of 75.
• Initiated the turnaround of financial services network from evaluation and design to completion. Implemented network management system.
• Delivered new packet-switching network that reduced network operation costs by 50 percent.

• EXPERIENCE (CONTINUED)

Engineering Manager, 1991 - 1994

- Established new department for inventory control, distribution, equipment testing/repair, and technical support.
- Developed and administered five-million-dollar budget.
- Hired and managed staff of 25.
- Started and structured production and inventory control departments to manage and control distribution of capital equipment inventory.
- Set up and reorganized a mini/micro computer equipment repair department to reduce company dependency on third-party services and improve operating cost.
- Created and implemented new personal computer and satellite-based financial service product that provided more information to clients at less cost.
- Redesigned product line to streamline production cost by 10 percent.
- Established technical support and training program, providing improved client retention and sales.

Indiana Bell Telephone Company, Indianapolis, Indiana, 1989 - 1991
Communications System Representative

- Provided technical assistance to national sales account teams.
- Used computer aided designs systems in developing total data communications systems for clients.

• EDUCATION

B.S.E.E. Electrical Engineering
Illinois Institute of Technology
Chicago, Illinois 60616

• REFERENCES

Professional references will be provided on request.

Donald E. Henry

3125 Cool Creek Drive • Carmel, IN 46032 • D.Henry@xxx.com • 317-555-9406

Objective	To obtain a position as an engineer with the opportunity to apply my knowledge of digital circuit design, programmable controllers, and microprocessors.
Employment	**Systems Engineer, July 2003 to present** **Allied Wholesale Electrical Supply Inc.** **Indianapolis, IN**

Responsibilities include:
- Resolving computer problems
- Keeping inventory
- Working with programmable controllers
- Working with CAD
- Analyzing change requests
- Writing troubleshooting documentation

Die Detailer, August 1999 to June 2003
Webber Engineering
Carmel, IN

Responsibilities included:
- Drawing and dimensioning die details
- Making engineering changes to die drawings
- Running blueprints

Education

Lawrence Institute of Technology, Southfield, MI
B.S. Electrical Engineering, 1999

Passed Professional Engineering Exam, June 1999

Patricia Allen

645 Green Street
Bloomington, IN 47403
(812) 555-8765
patriciaallen@xxx.com

Work History

2003-Present
CONSECO, INC./Indianapolis, IN
PROJECT MANAGER
➢ Prepare environmental assessments, facilities plans, specialized reports
➢ Collect data through research and field surveys
➢ Develop conceptual design of wastewater treatment plants

2000-2003
DUKE UNIVERSITY BOOKSTORE/Lafayette, IN
ASSISTANT BRANCH MANAGER
➢ Ordered stock
➢ Inventoried supplies
➢ Cleared and balanced daily sheets
➢ Supervised hourly employees

Education

Purdue University, Lafayette, IN
Bachelor of Science in Public Affairs, 2002
Majors: Environmental Science and Environmental Affairs

Courses: Biology, Chemistry, Energy and the Environment, Environmental Techniques, Geology, Hydrogeology, Lake and Watershed Management, Law and Public Policy, Physics, Urban Development

References

Available

FREDERICK P. SROBLEWSKI

3456 MUSCATEL AVENUE   TUCSON, ARIZONA 85718
FRED.SROBLEWSKI@XXX.COM   (602) 555-6543

BACKGROUND

Award-winning technical educator and computer support professional with international experience. Able to make an outstanding contribution to your organization in areas of:

• Management Information Systems
• Technical Education
• Technical Writing
• Computer Systems Support

SELECTED QUALIFICATIONS

TECHNICAL TRAINER - Achieved outstanding recognition as an educator. Selected and supervised staff of instructors.

CREATOR AND DEVELOPER - Researched, created, packaged, and implemented training programs never before taught in areas of quality management, computer hardware, computer software, and concepts from ideas/needs to systems application.

TECHNICAL WRITER - Track record of writing program manuals, self-taught programs, and on-the-job training manuals. Served as resource to writing staffs to evaluate and rewrite material for practical instruction.

INCREASED REVENUES - Because of personal excellence in providing training for both foreign and domestic clients, additional training services were purchased in multiple modules of $100K plus.

COMPUTER SUPPORT SPECIALIST - Comprehensive experience regarding computer hardware troubleshooting and repair of equipment, maintenance of integrated systems from mainframe to micro, including peripherals, used throughout the industry.

EDUCATION

U.S. Army Electronic Training, 1991 - 1994
• Achieved highest score of any student during 15-year existence of school.

SELECTED CAREER ACHIEVEMENTS

TRAINING SPECIALIST, JOHN ZINK COMPANY, 1998 - PRESENT
- Create, develop, and conduct training for both employees and customers in formal and informal settings.
- Evaluate courses to determine quality of content and format as well as recommend selection of appropriate staff trainers.
- Was directly used as instructor with clients in the U.S. and ten other countries.

TECHNICAL TRAINER, U.S. ARMY, 1990 - 1998
- Responsible for training theory and application of electronics to nontechnical personnel, resulting in exceptional number of participants being assigned to technical responsibilities.
- Responsible to provide total systems support under all conditions for assigned duty, with a battlefield support system.

SPECIAL TRAINING AND EXPERTISE

- Special Purpose Computers
- Super Computer Integrated Systems
- Mainframes through Micros
- Peripheral Equipment
- Personal Computer Applications

REFERENCES

Furnished upon request.

EARLE F. ABLE

6255 Maple Drive • Chicago, IL 60636
earleable@xxx.com • Telephone (312) 555-4948
Cell (312) 555-4897

OBJECTIVE

To attain a position as a designer drafter with a highly aggressive,
goal-oriented architectural engineering firm.

SKILLS

Design and Detailing of Commercial, Mechanical, Electrical,
and Plumbing Systems

Architectural Plan and Details and Site Layout

EXPERIENCE

ENGINEERING DEVELOPMENT DESIGN
May 1998 - Present
Position: Designer Drafter

Duties: Design development of mechanical, electrical, and plumbing
systems within commercial projects. Produce final bid documents on
multiple medias and AutoCAD software. Develop construction details
for architectural and engineering concepts. Also responsible for
pictorial sections used in development and layout.

EDUCATION

B.S. in Mechanical Engineering Technology
University of Illinois, Champaign, 1998

A.S. in Mechanical Design and Drafting Technology
Indianapolis Community College, 1996

REFERENCES

Furnished upon request

Curriculum Vitae
MARK STEVEN TRAVERS

Office Address
Computer Science Department
University of Dayton
Dayton, OH 45469
(513) 555-8976
marktravers@xxx.com

Employment Objective

A faculty position at a moderate- to small-size school that provides opportunities for both interaction with students and professional development.

Education

University of Cincinnati, Cincinnati, OH

Ph.D. in Computer Science, June 1998
Title: Combined Procedures Program
Advisor: Professor Richard Day
Qualifiers passed: Programming Languages, Operating Systems, and Artificial
                Intelligence
Minor Concentration: Mathematics

M.S. in Computer Science, December 1995

B.S. with highest honors in Computer Engineering, May 1993

Dissertation

(Combined Procedures Program)

This dissertation develops several semantics-based algorithms for integrating multiple variants of a program. The goal of such algorithms is to determine whether the changes in these variants conflict and, if they do not, to create an integrated program whose behavior is guaranteed to incorporate the changed behavior of the variants. Previous semantics-based algorithms have dealt with single procedure programs. However, integration of algorithms for realistic languages must deal with programs containing more than one procedure. The dissertation describes several semantics-based algorithms for integrating multiple procedure programs.

Dissertation (continued)

The goal of such analysis is to answer questions such as "Which statements affect the execution at a particular statement in a program?" and "Which statements are affected by the execution of a particular statement in a program?" Answers to these questions are useful in software maintenance, program debugging, and automatic program parallelization.

Research Interests

Programming environments and code generation for reduced instruction set architectures.

Professional Experience

University of Cincinnati, Cincinnati, OH
Computer Science Department
Research Assistant, June 1998 - Present
Conducted research, including thesis research, under the direction of Dr. Robert Roberts.

University of Cincinnati, Cincinnati, OH
Teaching Assistant, September 1996 - May 1998
Developed and gave lectures, prepared and graded both assignments and exams for an introductory course in Computer Programming (CA 302).

University of Dayton, Dayton, OH
Manager of Software Engineering, September 1994 - July 1996
Directed a staff of three to five programmers in the development of network software for the management school's local area network.

University of Dayton, Dayton, OH
Computer Engineering Department
Teaching Assistant, August 1990 - December 1994
Prepared and graded assignments for a junior level course in programming methodology (ECMP 998).

Additional Teaching Experience

Basic Computer Literacy Seminar, Indianapolis, IN
Instructor, June 1988 - July 1990
Instructed the teachers of the Dayton Catholic School System in the teaching of computer programming.

Technical Reports

Program Integration for Languages with Procedure Calls.
Technical report in preparation, Computer Science Department, University of Cincinnati, Cincinnati, OH.

Combined Procedures Theorem. Technical Report 990, Computer Science Department, University of Cincinnati, Cincinnati, OH.

Combined Procedures Graphs. Technical Report 997, Computer Science Department, University of Dayton, Dayton, OH.

Professional Societies

Association for Computing Machinery
Tau Beta Pi (Engineering Honor Society)

References

Professor Stan Silvers
Computer Science Department
University of Cincinnati
453 Victory Parkway
Cincinnati, OH 45221-0091

Professor Richard Day
Computer Science Department
University of Cincinnati
453 Victory Parkway
Cincinnati, OH 45221-0091
(513) 555-9975

Harold K. Kent
131 Palm Drive   Valparaiso, IN 46483
(219) 555-2232   HaroldKent@xxx.com

Summary

Seven years of marketing and sales experience with a proven record of success. Solid business management background in printing industry including both operations and supervision. Excellent skills in planning and organizing along with outstanding ability in sales with a strong technical background.

Education

Bachelor of Science, Biology/Computer Science
Rochester Institute of Technology, Rochester, NY, 1996

Experience

1996 - Present

Eli Lily and Company
Indianapolis, IN
Performance and Capacity Planning
Responsible for maintaining target performance levels on IBM 3090 systems using SMF, RMF, Omegamon, and other performance monitors. Also responsible for generating projected growth and capacity requirements.

Summer 1992

Eli Lily and Company
Indianapolis, IN
Systems Programmer
Responsible for system installation, generation, and maintenance using CBIIPO, SMP/E, and ISPF. Equipment: IBM 4381, 3090 processors. Operating systems: MVS/SP, MVS/XA, MVS/ESA.

Use of IBM utility programs - AMASPZAP, IEBUPDTE

Summer 1990

Eli Lily and Company
Indianapolis, IN
Applications Programmer
Responsible for creation of programs written in COBOL to specifications of user departments—accounting and payroll.

References

On request

Leslie Ryan

5391 Southward Plaza
Chicago, IL 60631
(312) 555-9008
leslie.ryan@xxx.com

Job Objective

Systems programming or applications programming of a technical nature.

Education

Graduated Rensselaer Polytechnic Institute, Troy, NY, in May of 1999 with a B.S. in Computer Science.

Experience

June 2002 - present
Computer Works, Carmel, IN
  Analyst - Responsible for the designing, coding, testing, and support of utility software products for the MVS/TSO environment. These products include the TSO/Superset-Utilities, FSE+I Host Storage and Tetrievall and Almost-TSO. All coding on these products has been in 370 Assembly Language.

Summer 2001
Butler University, Indianapolis, IN
  Instructor of Computer Science - Responsible for teaching Introduction to Computing, Structured Programming, Assembly Language Programming, and FORTRAN Programming.

Computer Languages

370 Assembler, Pascal, FORTRAN, COBOL, BASIC, SQL, C++

References

Available upon request.

PAUL THOMAS

987 Chestnut Hill Road   (302) 555-9812
Newark, Delaware 19713   paulthomas@xxx.com

QUALIFICATIONS

Ten years' experience in Engineering and Construction Management

Registered Professional Engineer in Commonwealth of Delaware

EDUCATION

B.S. in Civil Engineering
University of Delaware, Newark, Delaware

WORK EXPERIENCE

Boss Corporation, 10/97 - Present
Newark, Delaware

Project Manager
Project: Glendale Shopping Center
Newark, Delaware
5.6-million-dollar, 64,000 SF shopping center including Food Lion,
Osco Drug Store, and Krogers along with 20 retail shops.

Project: Marion County Airport
Indianapolis, Indiana
6.2-million-dollar, 100,000 SF airport terminal building. Complete
weather-tight shell of reinforced concrete structure with brick veneer.

WORK EXPERIENCE *(cont.)*

Concrete Quality Control Supervisor
Responsibilities: Supervise 20 concrete lab technicians performing tests at an on-site aggregate and sand plant and field tests on shotcrete and concrete.

Lead Civil Engineer
Responsibilities: Supervise the five-member civil construction engineering department. Provide concrete engineering expertise for over one million cubic yards of concrete. Assist construction supervision with underground shaft and tunnel concrete placement and temporary structures design.

Chief Discipline Engineer
Responsibilities: Supervise 15 civil, electrical, and mechanical construction engineers.

REFERENCES

On request

Peter Joseph Little

354 Long Hill Road

Middletown, CT 06457

(203) 555-9998

peterlittle@xxx.com

OBJECTIVE

Seeking a rewarding and challenging position in operations or administration where I can utilize over 20 years' experience to meet corporate objectives and advance my career.

EDUCATION

INDIANA UNIVERSITY   Bachelor of Science
Bloomington, IN   Business - Accounting

CAREER SUMMARY

DELTA FAUCET COMPANY
Indianapolis, IN 46280

SALES REPRESENTATIVE, December 1996 - present
• Responsible for the follow-up on sales leads from needs analysis through to the close of sale.
• Designed and implemented telemarketing system and procedures to generate sales leads.

DIRECTOR OF OPERATIONS, January 1994 - December 1996
• Prepared monthly financial statements for management.
• Managed all accounting and processing via computer system.
• Developed procedures transaction flow regarding closed sales, purchases, invoicing, and installation.
• Trained personnel to assume routine accounting transactions involved with computer.
• Supervised and evaluated job performance of two employees.

CAREER SUMMARY (CONTINUED)

JOHNSON MEMORIAL HOSPITAL
Franklin, IN 46131

VICE PRESIDENT OF OPERATIONS, May 1990 - December 1994
• Started initial steps in replacing existing PC hardware in customer base.
• Directed initial stages of development on new Care Plan software module.
• Provided direction to all departmental supervisors for the growth of each department.

DIRECTOR OF OPERATIONS, September 1987 - April 1990
• Prepared yearly budget and monthly financial statements for management approval.
• Reviewed/summarized departmental activity for reporting to president.
• Involved with departmental heads in evaluation, review, education, and training of employees.
• Evaluated methods used in training new clients.

ADMINISTRATIVE ASSISTANT, June 1983 - September 1987
• Oversaw mainframe computer operations.
• Handled all company requisitions for products and supplies.
• Assisted in development of training procedures for new clients.
• Trained support staff on how to provide assistance to clients.

SALES REPRESENTATIVE, July 1981 - June 1983
• Solely responsible for the generation of sales leads for the service bureau.
• Evaluated prospects' needs and provided assistance in conversion to mainframe computer.

UNIVERSITY OF KENTUCKY
CAREER PLANNING AND PLACEMENT CENTER
LEXINGTON, KENTUCKY 40506

Angela Conrad

9867 High Drive • Lexington, KY 40506
A.Conrad@xxx.com • (415) 555-8712

Objective   A position in research and development with a company interested in wide applications of polymeric materials. Possibility for a move into management preferred.

Education   UNIVERSITY OF KENTUCKY, Lexington, KY
M.S., Chemical Engineering, 1999

LOUISIANA TECH UNIVERSITY, Ruston, LA
B.S., Chemical Engineering, 1997

Experience   7/98 - present
University of Kentucky
Dept. of Chemical Engineering
Lexington, KY
Research Assistant
Laboratory of Dr. S. Silverberg
Study structures formed by diblock copolymers in a solvent selective for one block. Use light, X-ray, and neutron scattering to determine micelle structure as a function of solution conditions. Compared the spherical micelles to structures predicted for multi-armed star polymers.

5/95 - 9/98
University of Kentucky
Dept. of Chemical Engineering
Lexington, KY
Research Assistant
Studied properties of mono-layer and multi-layer films of alkanoic acids and alkylsiloxanes on solid surfaces.

References   On request

~Megan E. Pierson

176544 Ventura Blvd.
Cleveland, Ohio 44136
(419) 555-9876
meganpierson@xxx.com

~EDUCATION

Ph.D. Inorganic/Organometallic Chemistry, 1998
Tufts University
Medford, Massachusetts

B.A. Major - Biochemistry and Chemistry, 1996
Kenyon College
Gambier, Ohio

~EMPLOYMENT

Postdoctoral Research Associate/Tufts University
Medford, Massachusetts
8/98 - Present
~ Catalyst testing for new synthetic routes and a product analysis.
  Extensive use of GC, GCIMS, and FT-NMR.

Analytical Chemist/Majestic Company
Huntington, Indiana
8/95 - 1/98
~ Method development and analysis of gas, liquid, and solid samples using
  GC and GC-MS.

Research Assistant/Tufts University
Medford, Massachusetts
9/93 - 8/95
~ Zeolites modification and characterization of their reaction chemistry
  with small molecules.

REFERENCES AVAILABLE

PATRICIA DENNIS

987 W. 44th Street • Cheyenne, WY 82001• (307) 555-9872
patriciadennis@xxx.com

PROFESSIONAL OBJECTIVE

Opportunity to demonstrate superior managerial ability and administrative decision-making skills in a stable growth environment.

SUMMARY OF QUALIFICATIONS

- Highly organized and motivated.
- Ability and patience to train and develop office staff - provide employees with the tools they require to reach expectations and achieve objectives.
- Thorough knowledge of computers - IBM PC, Lotus Notes, MS Office, Symphony Data Base, IBM 38, typing, 10-key by touch, dictaphone, two-way radio system.
- Extensive experience in all phases of construction accounting including contracts, legal aspects, bonding procedures.
- Good rapport with all levels of employees, corporate management, engineers, subcontractors, and public agencies.

EDUCATION

Fitchburg State College, Fitchburg, Massachusetts

SEMINARS

- Massachusetts Mechanics Lien Laws
- Insurance and Bonding

REFERENCES AVAILABLE

Maria Lynn White

28 Octavia Trace
Cincinnati, OH 45243
(513) 555-8673
mariawhite@xxx.com

CAREER OBJECTIVE

Safety Director, with specialization in compliance monitoring and disposal of hazardous materials.

EDUCATION

B.S. Health Sciences

Purdue University, 2000

Minor: Health Sciences

WORK EXPERIENCE

Currently Manager of Environmental Affairs, ENVIROCHEM, Cincinnati
Former Hazardous Materials Technician, UNIVERSITY OF CINCINNATI

DUTIES

- Maintained sample tracking files and manifests
- Directed government contract, Illinois military bases
- Inspected, reviewed, and selected TSD facilities
- Sampled and identified various solid and liquid waste streams
- Profiled materials and obtained MSDS sheets
- Completed manifests and land disposal restriction forms
- Coordinated transportation of hazardous materials
- Constructed Site Emergency Response (EPA & OSHA)
- Designed Hazard Communication Program
- Consulted for companies to maintain EPA/OSHA compliance
- Sorted and monitored decayed radioactive materials
- Tested and bulked characteristic flammables and corrosives

REFERENCES

On Request

■ MARGARET MARY STILES

904 West Street
Springfield, OH 45501
(987) 555-9876
margaretstiles@xxx.com

■ OBJECTIVE

To secure a challenging position in the field of environmental engineering

■ EDUCATION

M.S. in Environmental Engineering
Expected Graduation Date: December 2004
University of Pennsylvania, Philadelphia, Pennsylvania
GPA 3.75/4.0

B.S. in Civil Engineering - June 2001
Wittenberg University, Springfield, Ohio 45501

■ COURSES

- Advanced Water Supply and Sewerage
- Analysis of Receiving Water Quality
- Hydraulics and Fluid Mechanics Engineering
- Groundwater Pollution
- Biological Waste Treatment
- Water Resources Engineering
- Public Health Engineering

■ EXPERIENCE

RESEARCH ASSISTANT, January 2000 - Present
Civil Engineering Department
University of Pennsylvania
- Examining the applicability of the Advanced First Order Uncertainty Method to Water Quality Modeling including the Streeter-Phelps equation and QUAL2E.

COMPUTER LAB OPERATOR, September 1997 - December 1999
College of Engineering
University of Pennsylvania
- Helped users with systems-related and language-related problems. Maintained computer lab software and resources.

robert c. norton

596 Walean Drive • St. Paul, MN 55631
(612) 555-1213 • robertnorton@xxx.com

objective

To obtain a position as an operations research analyst in transportation, manufacturing, or consulting.

education

University of Minnesota, Minneapolis, MN
Master's Degree expected in June 2003 in Operations Research

Syracuse University, Syracuse, NY
Bachelor's Degree in June 2001 in Mathematics

experience

Multi-Food, Minneapolis, MN - Marketing, 4/01 - 8/03
- Analyzed supermarket scanner data to aid in marketing strategy for food products.

Allstate, New York Office
Corporate Finance, 5/99 - 4/01
- Created and analyzed financial models of insurance companies being considered as merger or acquisition candidates.
- Formulated transaction-cash-flow and financial projections of company operations.

Reliable Insurance Agency, Indianapolis, IN
Marketing, 5/97 - 5/99
- Performed pricing sensitivity analysis of recently developed life insurance products, using actuarial and financial principles.

credentials

- Actuarial exam passed, September 1997
- Computer skills: Lotus, APL, BASIC, Pascal, MS Office

references

On Request

Thomas Clegg

1311 S. Main • Brookings, SD 57006 • (605) 555-2934 • thomasclegg@xxx.com

Objective:

To obtain a position in computer software or systems design with interest in expert systems and object-oriented programming.

Education:

South Dakota State University (9/98 - 6/01)
Brookings, S.D.

> B.S. Computer Systems Engineering (an interdisciplinary major combining computer science and electrical engineering)

Employment History:

Associate Programmer Intern (6/01 - Present)
Accufact Systems, Inc., Kansas City, MO

> *Working on two projects. Designing a C program to download, manipulate, and transmit data between IBM mainframes (developed on IBM PS/2 with HLLAPI). Designing an expert systems knowledge base to automate generation of report request files on IBM system.*

Technical Support Specialist (3/98 - 6/99 and 9/99 - 6/01)
Academic Information Resources, South Dakota State University, Brookings, SD

> *Isolated and corrected problems on Ethernet and AppleTalk local area networks and network modem operations. Also performed setup and minor repair of terminals, microcomputers, and DEC and Sun workstations.*

Field Engineering Intern (6/97 - 9/97)
Illinois Public Service, Kankakee, IL

> *Engineered the maintenance and/or replacement of overhead and underground power distribution lines.*

Microcomputer Consultant (1/96 - 3/96)
Rand Computer Center, SDSU, Brookings

> *Answered questions involving IBM PC and Macintosh microcomputers.*

Software Engineering Intern (6/95 - 9/95)
Kankakee Journal, **Kankakee, IL**
Researched, designed, and implemented modified payroll system for production departments of newspaper.

Computer Skills:

Operating Systems: UNIX, Apple Macintosh, MS-WINDOWS, OS/X.

Languages: Pascal, C, C++, COBOL, Ada, Lisp, FORTRAN 68000 Assembly, and BASIC.

Expert Systems: VP Expert

IC DESIGN: VLSI System Design, Computer Architecture, Digital Design Laboratories.

REFERENCES AVAILABLE

Robert M. Nicholes

1987 Wembley Circle   Houston, TX 77058
Home (713) 555-9876   Cell (713) 555-4897   robertnicholes@xxx.com

Employment History

Employer	Position	Dates
Clark Vocational Technical College, Houston, TX	CAD Supervisor	3/00 - Present
Target Stores, Inc. Minneapolis, MN	CAD Designer	3/99 - 3/00
College Life Insurance Company Dayton, OH	Computer Technician	2/97 - 3/99
Ohio Savings & Loan Cincinnati, OH	Computer Technician	9/95 - 2/97
CMS/Anacomp Indianapolis, IN	Computer Technician	2/94 - 9/95

Additional Training

Butler University	AutoCAD Course	2000
Texas Technical College	Drafting/CAD Technology	Currently enrolled

References

Furnished upon request.

Frederick J. Miller

5319 West Hill Drive
Lawrence, IN 46226
(317) 555-6740
frederickmiller@xxx.com

Objective   To obtain a position as editor or technical editor where my experience will be of value.

Experience   **Best Textbook Co., Chicago, IL**
Employed August 1992 to present

1999 - present   Senior editor of VCR facts manuals.
Technical service data for the repair of video cassette recorders by electronic technician.

1995 - 1999   Senior editor of computer facts manuals.
Technical service data for the repair of home and business microcomputers by electronic technician. Integral part of product development and start-up team.

1993 - 1995   Senior editor of quick facts manuals.
Quick reference television service manuals carried by electronic technicians in the field.

1992 - 1993   Compilation editor of counter facts documentation.
Cross-reference listing of individual major component to replacement part manufacturer's equivalent part. Eight major category divisions.

Education   B.S. degree in Computer Technology, 1992
Purdue University

RESUME SUBMITTED IN CONFIDENCE

REFERENCES AVAILABLE

Maria P. Wroblewski

3567 Hope Lane
Hanover, New Hampshire 03755
(603) 555-6786
mariawroblewski@xxx.com

Objective: Operations Manager

Education:

B.S. Computer Science
Northern Illinois University

Technical Summary:

Hardware: CPUS: AMDAHL 570, NAS 5000/7000, IBM 4341, 3081, 3090

Software: MUV/SP/XA, JES2, TSO/ISPF, SKSF, OS/DOS, JCL/UTILITIES, IDCAMS, CA7, RESOLVE, TMS, CICS, VM/CMS, PL/I, BASIC, EXEC2, OMEGAMON

Experience:

RCA, 3/99 - Present
New York, New York
Operations Manager

★ Coordinate data processing activities
★ Maintain and ensure the availability and reliability of a 300+gb multi-cup/os shared DASD environment
★ Set up and review DASD production runs (backups, archival, compaction, space release)
★ Write procedures for and train production personnel and operators
★ Generate solutions for system/production problems
★ Work with customers to resolve their programming needs
★ Fix JCL errors and programming errors
★ Set up and install PCs for customers

Experience (cont.):

Service Merchandise, 1/97 - 3/99
Minneapolis, Minnesota
Analyst

★ Key player in technical support team working with the
system programmer
★ Applied systems and helped with systems mods
★ Set up Xerox 9700, programming, creating JSL, FSL,
DJDE for Xerox laser printer
★ Helped maintain data center and was in charge of cor-
recting all JCL errors
★ Helped train computer operators on certain tasks

REFERENCES AVAILABLE

JILL NELSON

Current Address	**Permanent Address**
897 Burlington Ave.	5311 Rosalind, Apt. #3
Atlanta, GA 30319	Calumet City, IL 60409
(404) 555-9112	(708) 555-9991

OBJECTIVE

Seeking an applied research and development or manufacturing position in the field of material science.

EDUCATION

M.S. Materials Science & Engineering
Oglethorpe University - May 1998

B.S. Mechanical Engineering
University of California - 1996

EXPERIENCE

Research Assistant
Investigated the micromechanical as well as the macromechanical properties of a ceramic matrixceramic fiber composite. Prepared testing specimens and performed various mechanical testing schemes, including three- and four-point bending and tensile tests. Progress of the research was supervised by Dr. James Travers.

Lab Consultant
Helped students debugging programs written in FORTRAN.

Research Assistant
Investigated the possibility of two polymer systems being the precursor of a superconducting material. Various compositions of the polymer solutions were prepared and fibers were spun via several methods. High-temperature mechanical testings were carried out to determine the survivability of the fiber under pyrolysis.

REFERENCES AVAILABLE

John Robert Treat

1544 McCullough Court
Indianapolis, IN 46575
JR.Treat@xxx.com
(317) 555-9876

Skills

Experience working with clients, writing multi-task AutoLISP routines, third-party software such as D.C.A. and WILDSOFT, as well as complete menu customization. Ability to work on fast-paced schedules and short deadlines.

Education

Two years, Saint Lawrence University, Canton, NY
Math Major

AutoCAD Training - Level I and III
Ivy Tech, Indianapolis, IN
AutoLISP Programming, Diversified Graphic

Work Experience

CMW Inc., 1998 - Present
2345 Walden Place
Indianapolis, IN 46254

Job duties: preparation of site development construction drawings, layout and staking plans from architectural plans, boundary and land title surveys, as well as preliminary and final plans.

The following represent a portion of my project experience:

• Holiday Inn, Lafayette, IN
  Hotel complex for General Hotel Corporation
• Sam's Wholesale, Indianapolis, IN
  Wholesale warehouse for the WALMART Corporation
• Castleton Square, Indianapolis, IN
  Traffic signal modification and parking lot improvements
• Indianapolis Airport Authority apron repair and addition

REFERENCES ON REQUEST

NABIL GHALAYINI

1482 West Street • Des Plaines, IL 60018 • (847) 555-4049

OBJECTIVE

To obtain position in environmental and water resources engineering.

EDUCATION

B.S. in Civil Engineering
Tennessee Technological University, Cookesville, TN
Graduated 1996

EXPERIENCE

SDI Consultants, LTD., Oakbrook, IL
7/01 to Present

- Design stormwater management plans.
- Perform watershed studies, including hydraulic and hydrologic computer modeling of stream flow.
- Revise FEMA flood insurance studies.
- Deal extensively with federal, state, and local regulatory agencies in connection with stormwater and flood control issues.

Intern, ADCO West, V.V., Heemskerk, The Netherlands
6/00 to 9/00

- Computer assisted analysis and design of semi-submersible oil transports.

SKILLS

- Working knowledge of HEC and SCS computer models.
- Familiar with EPA HSPF model.
- Special interest in water pollution control, particularly stormwater quality management and quality control of groundwater supplies.

REFERENCES AVAILABLE

Charles D. Stiles

8765 South East Street

Ada, OH 45810

Charles.Stiles@xxx.com

(419) 555-9876

Career Objective

Position that requires technical knowledge in the areas of design, testing, and reliability of mechanical and electrical systems in order to produce a quality product.

Education

Ohio Northern University, Ada, OH
B.S. in Mechanical Engineering Technology, 1998

Ohio Northern University, Ada, OH
Have completed 21 hours of electronics and 15 hours of computer programming.

Work Experience

Shepherd Engineering - Tulsa, OK
2000 to Present
Responsibilities include:
- Component designs
- Thermoset and thermoplastic molding
- Tooling evaluation
- Assembly line setups
- Adhesive development
- Robot feasibilities
- Supplier contacts

Ford Motor Company - Detroit, MI
1998 to 2000
Responsibilities included:
- Traveling to various engineering facilities to develop tests
- Setting up inventory systems
- Maintaining budget
- Supervising laboratory technicians
- Publishing testing manuals and reports

References available

ALEXANDER HO

986 Parker Lane   Work (415) 555-2939
Walnut Creek, CA 94595   Home (415) 555-9875

SUMMARY

Intimate knowledge of microcomputer industry and applications software.
More than ten years of broad international business experience with a Fortune
500 corporation. Fluent in Mandarin Chinese, good command of Japanese and
Thai.

Accomplishments in:

• Feasibility Studies
• Office Automation
• Multinational Manufacturing Analysis and Control
• Economic Recovery and Product Positioning and Pricing
• Marketing Plans and Strategies
• Strategic Planning and Competitive Analysis

EXPERIENCE

HOCORP INTERNATIONAL, INC., WALNUT CREEK, CA
1994 - Present
President
> Founded consulting and marketing firm to evaluate business problems,
> determine software requirements, and develop microcomputer systems
> to meet clients' needs.

INTERCORP INC., LOS ANGELES, CA
1993 - 1994
Manager, New Product Programs
> Responsible for product evaluation, assessment of marketing potential,
> and development of product feasibility studies.
>
> Completed feasibility study on 9500 Electronic Printing System for the
> Pacific Rim Area, led to the development of a new market area.
>
> Evaluated marketing strategies for microcomputer products in open-
> market countries.

INTERCORP (cont.)
1991 - 1993
Manager, Field Pricing

Developed, evaluated, and recommended strategic and tactical pricing actions enabling affiliates to exceed targeted profits.

Developed and implemented major account pricing strategy for Malaysia resulting in an increase in major accounts and a reduction in cancellations.

1987 - 1991
Manager, Commercial Analysis

Direct responsibility for long-range competitive forecast for group of 25 affiliates. Measured performance of current products, competitive practices, and identified risks and opportunities to business strategies.

EDUCATION

M.B.A. 1984   University of Georgia, Athens, GA

B.S.   1983   Notre Dame University, South Bend, IN
        Major: Industrial Administration

B.A.   1981   City College, Chicago
        Major: Marketing

• PETER SIMMONS

678 Park Street #546   Noblesville, IN 46060
P.Simmons@xxx.com   (219) 555-6042

• OBJECTIVE
To obtain an executive position in marketing with an emerging company that is dedicated to a long-term program.

• EXPERIENCE
• DCS SOFTWARE, INC. Noblesville, IN
Senior Partner, 5/95-Present
Contingency Marketing Agency

  ~ Designed marketing strategies for local and national companies
  ~ Directly responsible for meeting payroll of 25 full-time employees
  ~ Improved sales for one company by over 25% in a 12-month period
  ~ Developed marketing programs for corporations

• BLAUVELT ENGINEERS, New York, NY
Regional Sales Manager, 1/94-5/95
Business Communications Systems

  ~ Set regional sales record in six months
  ~ Procured 10 national accounts
  ~ Exceeded company goals for the 1994 fiscal year
  ~ Developed sales marketing program for the northwest regional area

• EDWARDS AND KELCEY, Livingston, NJ
Marketing Director, 8/90-1/94

  ~ Implemented international marketing program
  ~ Promoted from sales executive to marketing director
  ~ Company's sales increased over 100% in a 12-month span
  ~ Successful in developing databases

• EDUCATION
Stevens Institute of Technology, Hoboken, NJ
Bachelor of Arts Degree in the area of Technical Marketing Design

JAMES TRAVERS

1420 Douglas Drive • Indianapolis, IN 46032
J.Travers@xxx.com • (317) 555-1177

CAREER OBJECTIVE

A position in information systems with an industry leader that involves utilization of my management, system development, and engineering skills.

EDUCATION

Northwestern University, Evanston, IL
B.S. in Industrial Management, May 2002
Minors: Industrial Engineering/Computer Science

EXPERIENCE

Business Analyst, Southwestern Bell, 6/02 - Present
- Designed and developed purchasing module for corporate procurement system.
- Researched requirements for purchasing system.

Sales Engineer, Butler Engineering, Summers 2000, 2001
- Coordinated and conducted corporate expansion research and recommendations.
- Proposed and planned computer network and database development.
- Maintained project management documentation and Lime line.

Founding President, National Fraternity Chapter, 3/99 - 5/00
- Coordinated expansion effort with national headquarters.
- Oversaw allocation of budget in excess of $40,000.
- Organized collective efforts for MDA.

Publicity Director, Student Management Association, 8/99 - 5/00
- Coordinated advertising, marketing, and public awareness of SMA.
- Directed publicity for campus Career Day.

Executive Social Director, Northwestern Residence Hall, 1999
- Organized, planned and oversaw activities for 1,500 students.
- Enforced and negotiated hall policies with resident hall management.

REFERENCES

Available upon request

MARK HOMER
P.O. Box 22 • Boston, MA 02125 • M.Homer@xxx.com • (617) 555-9876

OBJECTIVE

Key executive position in marketing management or general management.

SUMMARY

Fifteen years of diverse, multidisciplinary management experience with broad-based exposure and expertise in the various facets of marketing, operations, sales, and general management.

EDUCATION

MBA (Marketing)   1995   University of Massachusetts
Master's (Mathematics) 1990   Williams College
B.B. (Mathematics)   1988   Williams College

EXPERIENCE

CADD CONVERSION, 1994 to Present
VICE PRESIDENT
DIRECTOR OF MARKETING

- Reversed the 25 percent decline in unit sales volume in the two-year period preceding employment. Increased unit sales volume 25 percent and total sales revenue 75 percent in the subsequent two-year period.

- Developed marketing strategies to exploit existing product opportunities in present and new markets, i.e., commercial, industrial, institutional, and plan/spec. Strategies focused on an expanded product line with exclusive options and different product features, multiple model selections, and complementary new products.

- Conceptualized and implemented an aggressive product diversification effort. Supplementary HVAC products were acquired on a representation basis and now comprise approximately 50 percent of total sales revenue.

- Established a national sales representation network to market industrial/commercial ceiling fans and air-handling, air-cleaning, heating, and ventilation equipment.

- Identified and developed private label accounts in three new markets, i.e., agricultural, church, and direct mail, resulting in a 25 percent increase in private label unit sales volume.

EXPERIENCE (cont.)
TECTONIC SOFTWARE SYSTEMS, 1990 to 1994
BUSINESS DEVELOPMENT MANAGER

- Identified and exploited complementary business opportunities in new but related markets resulting in a 15 percent increase in special OEM Bales.

- Devised a simplified marketing strategy to upgrade, restructure, and optimize the performance of mature strategic business units.

- Developed comprehensive business assessments relative to participation in high-growth, high-profit consumer and industrial product markets.

- Assumed a leading role in the identification, strategic assessment, and financial analysis of complementary business acquisitions.

MULTIFRAME, 1988 to 1990
MARKETING MANAGER
PRODUCT MANAGER

- Created a $25M new market by modifying an existing product to meet specific customer needs in the software system for Macintosh.

- Managed the successful launch of two new "engineered" products for the software industry and eliminated outdated product lines.

- Supervised an innovative and persuasive advertising/sales promotion program to create demand for engineered products at the OEM level and to exploit burgeoning after-market sales opportunities.

REFERENCES AVAILABLE

EDWARD DUMPHY

566 Perry Boulevard • Altus, Oklahoma 74170 • (918) 555-7809 • E.Dumphy@xxx.com

OBJECTIVE: FIELD ENGINEER
To manage heavy highway construction projects.

EDUCATION
Purdue University
Bachelor of Science, Construction Management, May 2002

RELATED COURSEWORK

Temporary Structures	Electrical/Mechanical Systems
Construction Equipment	Heavy Construction Estimating
Soils in Construction	Legal Aspects in Construction

EXPERIENCE
Project Engineer, 6/02 to Present
WILLIBROS BUTLER ENGINEERS, INC.

- Interstate 465 Widening Project; contract value $55 million.
- Responsible for internal and subcontractor pay-letter quality, subcontractor negotiations with the State of Oklahoma Department of Transportation, and subcontractor scheduling.
- Produced weekly and monthly cost/quality reports.
- Managed punch list and construction crews.
- Assisted Project Superintendent in selling of job.

Assistant Operations Manager, 5/00 to 6/02
ROCK WARE CONSTRUCTION COMPANY

- Responsible for residential demolition; installation of concrete footings, drywall, and painting.
- Performed concrete quantity takeoffs and job setup/preplanning.
- Honed practical understanding of construction problems.
- Developed teamwork skills.

Shipping and Receiving Coordinator, Summers 1998, 1999
WINDSOR SHIPPING COMPANY

- Responsible for all phases of shipping and receiving.
- Packaged merchandise and performed computerized inventory control.
- Processed purchase orders.
- Served as forklift operator, truck driver, and various clerical capacities.

REFERENCES AVAILABLE UPON REQUEST

PAUL THOMPSON

66 ADAMS HILL DRIVE   NEW ALBANY, IN 47150
(317) 555-9876   P.THOMPSON@XXX.COM

OBJECTIVE

SHORT-TERM GOAL: Managerial/supervisory level position applying CAD/GIS skills to meet employer's objectives.
LONG-TERM GOAL: Project manager.

WORK EXPERIENCE

GIS SPECIALIST, GANNETT FLEMING, 2000 - PRESENT
- Manage all digital mapping projects.
- Planimetric and contaminant plume mapping for major chemical company.
- Real estate site assessment reports.
- Marketing and service sales.

AUTOCAD MANAGER, BAKER ENGINEERING, 1999 - 2000
- Managed and supervised all AutoCAD projects.
- Developed marketing and CAD sales strategies.
- Responsible for AutoCAD production with respect to mechanical engineering.

C.P.M. ENGINEERS, 1995 - 1999
- Implementation of an Intergraph 400 DEC/VAX system.
- Responsibilities included CAD training of engineers and managers of graphic systems, data conversion programming, quality control, and system maintenance.

EDUCATION

B.A. Geography, Illinois State University, May 2000
M.S. expected, Geography, Indiana University S.E., May 2002
GIS Management Seminar, Indiana University, April 2001

ACHIEVEMENTS

- Gained a thorough knowledge of computer graphics through project involvement.
- Compiled land-use and transportation maps for Hamilton County Planning Commission.

REFERENCES ON REQUEST

Alandro Chavez

Campus Address   **Home Address**
8223 Green Street   93 West 4th Street
Pasadena, CA 91125   Long Beach, CA 90808
(818) 555-7879   (213) 555-9876

Education

B.S. in Civil Engineering, June 2003
California Institute of Technology, Pasadena, CA
GPA 3.67

Work Experience

PROJECT ENGINEER, Welding Corporation, August 2003 - Present

Main projects consisted of bridge redecking and finalizing the construction of a cut-and-cover tunnel. Responsibilities included:
• Coordination of all subcontractors and suppliers with JBC and DOT
• Scheduling weekly quantity surveys
• Estimating weekly budget reports
• Interpretation of drawings and specifications

ASSISTANT PROJECT MANAGER, Grote Construction, January 1996 - August 2003

Responsibilities included:
• Estimating costs
• Quantity takeoff
• Crew sizing and scheduling
• Job cost control subcontractor
• Quantity surveys
• Design and determination of construction methods

Honors and Affiliations

• Chi Epsilon (XE) National Civil Engineering Honor Society
• Dean's Honor List, College of Engineering
• American Society of Civil Engineers (ASCE)

Computer Skills

• Proficient with Macintosh and IBM computers, associated software programs.
• BASIC and Pascal programming, STRUDL, experienced in the NMSU mainframe.

JESSICA BISHOP

1165 Georgia Road • West Lafayette, Indiana 47906
(317) 555-9876 • J.Bishop@xxx.com

OBJECTIVE
To find a challenging position in the Aerospace Industry that would utilize my engineering skills.

EDUCATION
Embry-Riddle Aeronautical University, FL
Degree: Bachelor of Science in Aerospace Engineering

EXPERIENCE
January 2000 - present
Aeroflight International, Lafayette, IN
Title: Strength Engineer

Responsible for detailed stress analysis for engine components. Hand and Finite element methods were utilized to examine the structural adequacy of various components of the fan and core thrust reverse (fixed and translating parts), the composite inlet and accessory compartment doors, and the fixed fan duct. Analysis included static, thermal, and pressure loads in conformance with military standards. Interfaced closely with the design group during the preliminary release phase to accelerate and optimize drawings.

June 1996 - January 2000
Commercial Aircraft Program
Title: Value Engineer

Assigned to training program to interface with manufacturing. Goal of the project was to discover fabrication techniques and difficulties and to improve channels of communication between engineers and manufacturing personnel. Concepts of value engineering were used on selected intensive and repeating problems. The project chosen was the air-conditioning system for the midsize commercial aircraft. Cost savings realized through this program were considerable.

May 1993 - June 1996
Elite Aerospace Systems, Desert Palms, CA
Title: Stress Engineer

Responsible for engineering analysis and structural substantiation on modifications for various commercial aircraft. Worked closely with FAA Designated Engineer Reps (DER) in design support work.

COMPUTER EXPERIENCE
FEM programs such as NASTRAN, PATRAN, and PIPELINE on both VAX and IBM.

MUHAMAD JULI-ADMERE

6543 Maple Street ▌ Greenwood, IN 46142
Phone: 317-555-1123 ▌ *E-mail: m.admere@xxx.com*

EDUCATION

▌ B.S. Geology; Miami University - Oxford, Ohio - 2002
▌ Graduate Studies in Geology; Oberlin College - Oberlin, Ohio
▌ Forestry and Natural Resources; Ohio Northern University - Ada, Ohio
▌ OSHA 29 CFR 1910.120 Training

PROFESSIONAL EXPERIENCE

Project Geologist, Computers & Structures, Inc., April 2002 - present

▌ Responsibilities include managing over 200 environmental assessments for properties undergoing acquisition or refinancing.

▌ Supervision and documentation of underground storage tank removal and closure and subsequent contaminated soil remediation.

▌ Responsible for remedial investigations including subsurface investigations to delineate the extent of soil contamination, design and installation of monitoring well systems, groundwater sampling and analysis, soil gas surveys and geophysical studies.

▌ Design of soil venting systems, groundwater recovery/treatment systems and bioremediation programs.

▌ Project management responsibilities including proposals, drill scheduling, material purchasing, invoicing, and client development.

AFFILIATIONS

▌ Ohio Academy of Science

▌ Geological Society of America

References are available and will be furnished upon request.

PATRICIA M. SPLIER

22 Westchester Drive • New Brunswick, New Jersey 08903
Patricia.splier@xxx.com • (201) 555-9000

OBJECTIVE

Capitalize on my experience in surveying and develop new skills in related fields.

EDUCATION

RUTGERS/COOK COLLEGE - New Brunswick, New Jersey
Awarded Bachelor of Science Degree in Earth Science, May 1998.

SUMMARY

Self-reliant and ambitious employee. Strongest assets include positive attitude, ability to work with and motivate others, ability to listen and learn quickly

AREAS OF KNOWLEDGE

Physical Geography	Meteorology
Chemistry	Maps/Map Reading
Structural Geology	Geomorphology
Botany	Glacial Geology
Mineralogy	Petrology
Wave Optics	Ecology

WORK EXPERIENCE

5/00 - Present

Parsons Brinckerhoff, New York, New York 10119
Party Chief

Responsible for six- to ten-person crews and knowledge-able in areas involving applied techniques of new subdivisions, construction layout, property, grade work, roads, boundary surveys, and stakeouts.

3/98 - 5/00

Matcor, Inc., New Brunswick, New Jersey
Assistant Surveyor

Involved field experience using theodolite and transit, aerial photographs, tax maps and deeds, sophisticated field instruments. Office work included computations with HP T41 computer and drafting of field information.

REFERENCES

Additional references furnished upon request.

CURRICULUM VITAE   **RYAN FARRELL**

Office Address   Home Address
Computer Science Department   876 Crestwood Drive
University of Virginia   Charlottesville, VA 22903
Charlottesville, VA 22903   (804) 555-5958

PRINCIPAL AREAS OF INTEREST

Programming Languages, Software Engineering, Operating Systems, Programming Environments, and Real-Time Process Control.

TEACHING AND RESEARCH EXPERIENCE

1996 - PRESENT   Ph.D. candidate in Computer Science, University of Virginia

Currently employed as research assistant by Professor L. Gisler. Thesis topic: Five-dimensional representations of four-dimensional programming languages. Principle areas of research: Software engineering and applied semantics.

PRESENTATIONS:
- A departmental seminar at the University of Virginia, Fall 2000
- Special ACM workshop on parellelism in four-dimensional languages, Spring 2000
- University of Virginia, June 1999
- Far West Symposium on Programming Languages and Systems, Fall 1998

TEACHING (C.S.-RELATED):
- Supervised programming languages seminar, Spring 1997
- Developed and taught first-year student orientation course, Fall 1996
- Class covered UNIX and HP program development utilities and programming methodology

TEACHING AND RESEARCH EXPERIENCE (CONT.)

LECTURING (C.S.-RELATED):
- Various lectures on denotational semantics three straight years (Foundations of Languages)
- Two lectures on overloading (Compilers)
- Three lectures on five-dimensional program graphs (Compilers and Optimization)

CONSULTING:
Consulted with individuals at College of William and Mary, Fall 2000, about algorithm for parallelizing four-dimensional languages.

POST-M.S. COURSEWORK:
- Undergraduate algorithms, combinalorics, abstract, algebra, and logic
- Graduate logic, theory of computation, and theory of programming languages
- Other: (informal) programming languages seminar (Fall 1996 - Spring 2000)
- Class projects included interpreting for a subset of ML, typechecking for a subset of ML, and implementing a scheduling algorithm by Cabow

TEACHING (NON-C.S.-RELATED):
- Assistant Instructor, Lifeguard Training
  University of Virginia, Phys. Ed. and Dance Department (Fall 2000)
- Assistant Instructor, Swimming
  University of Virginia, Phys. Ed. and Dance Department (Spring 2000)
- Assistant Instructor, Advanced Lifesaving
  University of Virginia, Phys. Ed. and Dance Department (Spring 2003)

Teaching and Research Experience (cont.)

Honors:
University of Virginia, Fellowship, 1999

Coursework:
Undergraduate: compilers, databases, and computer architecture
Graduate: compilers, databases, architecture, operating systems, and artificial intelligence
Graduate: special seminar on transformational programming

Class projects included two compilers (one for an ADA-like language), a small relational database, a simulation of a memory-resident database, a design for a CPU, a proposal for a new architecture, and a survey paper on scheduling theory.

Computer-Related Work Experience

1993 - 1999

Programmer analyst, systems analyst, Stemco Inc., Charlottesville, VA

Worked with the bar division's process control group. Primary responsibility was the Bruin 1/15, a PDP-11-based computer that controlled the widget furnaces:

- Troubleshot the Bruin 1/15 operating system
- Developed loadable communications link from the 1/15 to a PDP 11/45
- Troubleshot users' programs
- Rewrote University of Virginia's plot software
- Developed a software-development environment for the 1/15 that ran under DEC's RSX 11/M operating system
- Environment included simulation of parts of the 1/15 operating system and downline-loading software for Bruin 1/15 source code

OTHER PROGRAMMING WORK AT UNIVERSITY OF VIRGINIA

1988 - 1993
- Developed a single-user operating system for an 8090-based computer
- Developed an overlayed FORTRAN operator interface program for RSX-II/M
- Acquired, installed, and maintained programming tools from the DEC users group (DECUS)

1986 - 1987   **Programmer, University of Virginia**

- Wrote report-generating programs for the Alumni Office
- The Alumni Office's database, a hierarchical, UNIX-based database, was developed at the University of Virginia

RESEARCH REFERENCE

Professor Les Gisler
Computer Science Department
University of Virginia
Charlottesville, Virginia 22903
Les.Gisler@xxx.com
(804) 555-7787

------ *MARY ELLEN BOYD* ------

Current Address
P.O. Box 45
Medford, MA 02155
(617) 555-6543

Permanent Address
65 Fairbanks Drive
Carmel, IN 46032
(317) 555-9843

Mary.Boyd@xxx.com

Objective: To obtain a position in the field of product design, emphasizing product development or improvement and utilizing illustration, model-making, and other related skills.

Education: B.A. History/B.S. General Engineering
Tufts University, Medford, MA
Expected graduation: June 2004

Relevant Coursework:
- Calculus and Differential Equations
- Physics
- Materials Science
- Stress Analysis
- Software Engineering
- Technology and Aesthetics
- Electronics
- Industrial Design
- Manufacturing and Design
- Marker Rendering and Mechanical Drawing
- Statistics
- Computer Graphics and Design

Experience: **Manufacturing Engineer**
Revcorp Manufacturing, Carmel, IN
June 2002 to September 2002

- Provided technical support to electronics section.
- Designed tools for use in semi-rigid and flexible cable manufacturing area.
- Developed plans for implementation of purchased capital equipment and determined operating procedures for equipment.

Production Controller
Revcorp Manufacturing, Carmel, IN
June 2001 to September 2001

- Worked in product engineering and manufacturing section as an assistant planner.
- Distributed electrical part kits to workers for assembly.
- Verified parts lists from engineering drawings.
- Used Lotus 1-2-3 to track daily status of project subassemblies.

Freelance Designer
September 2001 to Present

- Produce graphic art, by hand and computer aided, for student organizations and other groups.
- Use Macintosh graphics to produce pins and shirts.

References: Available

Adam Cantor

Work Address   **Permanent Address**
Department of Chemistry   2141 Rock Street
University of Vermont   Alameda, CA 94504
Burlington, VT 16901   A.Cantor@xxx.com
602-555-9811   602-555-1123

Objective

To obtain a position as a senior research and development chemist in the fields of polymer or physical chemistry.

Education

Ph.D., Chemistry, University of Vermont, 2001
"Dynamic Light Scattering Study of Ternary Polymer Solutions"

B.S., Chemistry, Middlebury College, 1994
Minors: Mathematics, Physics

Experience

Research Assistant, June 1995 to January 2001
University of Vermont, Department of Chemistry

➤ Studied semi-dilute poly (n-alkyl isocynate) solutions containing a linear polystrene probe polymer.
➤ Examined concentration, molecular weight, and temperature dependencies of the ternary solutions.
➤ Performed dynamic and static light scattering measurements. Characterized solutions using FTIR, UV, viscometry, and differential refractory.
➤ Assisted in design, assembly, and maintenance of experimental instruments.
➤ Administered laboratory computer systems (UNIX, VMS, Macintosh, MS/DOS)

Experience (cont.)

Health and Safety Representative, February 1996 to January 2001
University of Vermont, Department of Chemistry

➤ Implemented laboratory safety measures, prepared chemical
inventories, and provided personal safety instructions.
➤ Aided in development of departmental safety film.

Teaching Assistant, June 1993 to December 1993
Middlebury College, Department of Chemistry

➤ Physical Chemistry, Laboratory (Head TA and Course TA)
➤ First-year Chemistry, Organic Chemistry

Honors

➤ Member, Eta Kappa Nu Fraternity
➤ Recipient, Chemical Engineering Scholarship of America
➤ National Merit Scholar

References

Furnished on Request

Felicitas Ortiz

55 West Green Street

Greenwood, IN 46143

Felicas.Ortiz@xxx.com

(317) 555-4456

Objective: To obtain employment within your company with the possibility of future advancement.

Experience: **Estimator/Designer, August 2002 - present**
Day's Lumber Company, Lebanon, IN
- Prepare takeoffs of roof and floor trusses for single and multifamily dwellings as well as commercial and institutional structures.
- Work requires the ability to read and understand all types of architectural drawings, and to develop a working roof or floor design that meets the owner's budget.
- Work involves serving the needs of both the sales department and the technical service engineers.

Estimator/Drafter/Computer Operator,
August 2000 - August 2002
B&B Builders Inc., South Bend, IN
- Estimated and designed custom homes and developed an estimating method using the computer to increase the efficiency and accuracy of residential estimating.

Education: **ITT Technical Institute, Indianapolis, IN**
Graduated from the Associate Degree program in Architectural Engineering Technology with honors, 2000.

Courses included classes in Technical Math, Physics, Estimating, Basic Engineering, and Architectural Drawing.

References Available

Darren Brown

1980 Dumont Drive • Houston, TX 77069
Darren.Brown@xxx.com • (713) 555-6979

Objective

A developer/ programmer position in a team-oriented, dynamic, creative software firm.

Education

Bachelor of Science, 1999, Tufts University - Medford, Massachusetts
Double major in political science and computer science

Experience

8/01 to present, Dodson & Associates, Inc., Houston, TX
QA Engineer: Designed and implemented test plans for Viewstar's document management software. Worked independently on varying hardware including Sony optical drive, Vidar scanners, Veresatee plotters, and Fuji printers and scanners all based around a standard PC/AT platform and Novell network.

1/00 to 8/01, Blauvelt Engineers, East Orange, NJ
Senior Coder: Maintained a Macintosh network under Apple Net and assisted students with the use of math lab software.

7/99 to 1/00, Congressman Dan Burton's Office, Washington D.C.
Research Assistant: Worked closely with Congressman's professional staff in preparing reports, constituent mail, press releases, and mailings.

9/98 to 6/99, Tufts Library, Medford, MA
Bibliographic Researcher: Located and traced volumes on a variety of national databases.

6/98 to 9/98, Hubbell, Roth & Clark, Inc., Bloomfield, MI
Legal Assistant: Interviewed expert witnesses, produced page-line summaries, and aided in all manner of legal tasks. Promoted to paralegal during mid-August.

Additional Information

- Fluent in C, C++, Pascal, Harvard Business Graphics
- Familiar with Prolog, Lisp, Smalltalk, and Ada
- Fluent in Spanish

Patrick Douglas Crowe

1632 Eastwood Lane
Charlottesville, VA 21320
PatCrowe@xxx.com
304-555-8710

Objective

Seeking continued employment in an expansive corporate environment involving data processing. Wish to formulate/utilize a wide variety of programming software for multiple applications. Desire opportunities that provide a career with professional growth and advancement.

Qualifications and Experience

August 1999 - Present
Programmer/Analyst, St. Frances Hospital, Granger, VA

Presently help develop and maintain computerized applications for all facets of this counseling/mental health center. Early duties involved rewriting the accounts receivable system to accompany altered file structures and access methods. Am presently concentrating on centralized scheduling system, exclusively the subsystem involving group therapy sessions, and am developing other programs to assist in current company reorganization. Also perform system operator and minor workstation troubleshooting duties as needed/able.

July 1995 - July 1999
Systems Analyst, Wilshire Design and Construction, Charlottesville, VA

Duties involved programmer/user functions for departmental budgeting, manufacturing, and analytical applications; performing life cycle cost analyses, using several patented models; and computing numerous space predictions for specific contracted projects. Major contributions included writing a BASIC program, which calculated contracts by worker-months and gave yearly summaries by labor grade and user-selected groupings.

Computer Expertise

Have experience or exposure to BASIC, FORTRAN, Clarion, Motorola 68000 Assembler. Also have knowledge in Wang Speed 11, Wang VS65, MVS/XA, Macintosh, and Lotus spreadsheets.

Education

Ball State University, Muncie, IN
B.S., Mathematics (Option Statistics), 1995
Minors: Music Theory and Computer Science

Yuki Osamika

765 5th Street
Washington, DC 20016
Yuki.Osamika@xxx.com
202-555-2213

Objective

Full-time position in telecommunications research and development, preferably in optical fiber networks, satellite communications, or antenna design.

Education

Currently pursuing Master of Science in Electrical Engineering with a concentration in telecommunications and fiber optics.
University of Washington, Expected Graduation: June 2003

Bachelor of Science with Highest Distinction in Electrical Engineering, Whitman College, May 2001

Experience

University of Washington, Dept. of Electrical Engineering, 2002 - 2003

Teaching Assistant: Controls courses and Introduction to Electronics lab.

Naylor Pipe Company, Chicago, IL, Summer 2001

Senior Staff Technologist: Conducted research on optical fiber communication systems. Primary research was an experimental study of privacy and security issues, fiber-to-the-home networks.

Amoco, Washington, DC, Summer 2000

Special Technical Assistant: Installed hardware and software for computer control test equipment, conducted stress tests on circuit boards, and wrote software to capture and plot oscilloscope waveforms.

References Available

-------- Hector Martinez --------

6285 Barfield Rd. • Atlanta, GA 30328 • H.Martinez@xxx.com • (404) 555-9648

Goal

Seeking a challenging position in statistical analysis/related fields.

Employment History

Summer 2002
Archer's Meat Packing, Fisher, IN
Cleanup person/Meat packer
• Responsible for ensuring the sanitary conditions of the plant for each day's use.

Summer 2001
Tyner's Farm, Carmel, IN
Farmworker
• Responsible for daily activities involving the various aspects of farm production and maintenance.

Summer 2000
Marion County Fair, Indianapolis, IN
Maintenance Worker
• Duties included preparing display buildings, completing construction repairs, and maintenance.

Summer 1999
Summers State Fair, Indianapolis, IN
Detassler
• Gained experience and proficiency and was put in charge of checking the work of 20 to 25 employees, as well as reporting to the employer.

Academic Qualifications

Bachelor of Science in Mathematics, Minor in Economics
Rose-Hulman Institute of Technology
May 2003

Pertinent Coursework

- Statistical Methods
- Operations Research
- Discrete and Combinatorial Algebra
- FORTRAN
- Calculus
- Numerical Analysis
- Linear Algebra
- Rose-Hulman Scholarship Recipient
- Probability

Personal Attributes

- Hardworking, with an excellent academic background and a dependable employment history.

- Take pride in work and eager to take on new responsibilities with the intention of seeing every project to a successful completion.

References Available

Curriculum Vitae
Victor Garcia
Professor in Engineering

Address:	6425 Eden Forest Drive, Victoria, Canada M2C 5X7
Telephone:	International 353-61-8896
Telefax:	International 353-61-8097

Languages: English
German (functional)

Education: University of Dublin, Ireland
Received degree 1983
Bachelor of Science Engineering (Mechanical)

Qualifications: Registered Professional Engineer
Association of Professional Engineers of Dublin University
February 1985

Experience: **Department of Natural Resources and Energy, Victoria, Canada**
February 1992 to present
Senior Engineer, Energy Branch

Responsible to the director of the Energy Branch for the implementation of federal-provincial energy agreements and of the provincially sponsored initiatives primarily in energy management, renewable energy development, and delivery of energy programs. Also responsible for the direction of technical staff, private and public sector, energy advisory services, and interdepartmental and interprovincial committee representation involving research and development, standards development, etc.

Department of Natural Resources and Energy, Victoria, Canada
February 1991 to February 1992
Acting Director, Energy Branch

Responsible to the Assistant Deputy Minister of Minerals and Energy to manage the Energy Branch with the responsibilities of supervising, coordinating, and participating in the formulation, implementation, and evaluation of government strategies regarding energy source development in Victoria.

Experience (cont.): **Energy Secretariat, Vancouver, Canada**
January 1988 to January 1991
Director, Conservation & Alternate Energy Branch

Responsible to the Deputy Minister for the planning and management of all work related to conservation and alternate energy. This included the implementation of federal-provincial agreements in these fields, planning and delivery of energy programs, evaluation of complex project proposals, administration of contracts, supervision and direction of technical support staff and energy consultants, liaison with the private sector and other levels of government, and advising private and public sector officials on energy and energy management matters.

Additional responsibilities involved general office management including space allocation, building maintenance, library and filing systems, computer equipment, etc.

Energy Secretariat, Vancouver, Canada
December 1986 to December 1987

Assisted in the implementation of a program for the demonstration of conservation and renewable energy technologies throughout Vancouver, Canada. The work included liaison with applicant on potential proposals for development and demonstration of projects, technical evaluation of such proposals with recommendations for funding levels and conditions of implementation, and inspection of the projects throughout the province.

The proposal evaluation process involved considerable liaison with the federal government, other government departments and agencies, and private consultants. Review of project final reports and other published information was also a responsibility.

**Related Training
and Experience:**

- Senior Member of Association of Energy Engineers
- Attendance at a wide variety of energy-related seminars, workshops, and training programs
- Participation in management training programs
- Representation of the province on the Northeast International Committee of Energy (NICE)

References: Available upon request

Samuel Broady

9876 Coring Drive
Northglenn, CO 80233
Sam.Broady@xxx.com
803-555-9876

Objective

A position in research and development in the fields of thin film technologies.

Education

Boston University, Boston, MA
M.S., Materials Science and Engineering

Saint John's College, Annapolis, MD
B.S., Ceramic Engineering

Experience

June 2000 - Present
Boston University, Department of Materials Science and Engineering.
• *Involved in design and building a sputtering chamber.*

June 1997 - June 2000
Saint John's College, Department of Ceramic Engineering
Annapolis, MD

Credentials

Computer Languages: BASIC, FORTRAN

Foreign Languages: Chinese

Additional

Member, Science and Engineering Associate

Recipient, Inroads Academic Achievement Award

John Mitchell

Present Address	**Permanent Address**
1325 Almond Street	223 Maple Drive
Bloomington, IN 47401	Carmel, IN 46032
(812) 555-9874	(317) 555-8975

Objective

Field Engineer - to manage heavy highway construction projects

Education

Bridgeport Engineering Institute, CT
Bachelor of Science, Construction Management, June 2000
Minor: Business Administration

Related courses

Temporary Structures
Construction Equipment
Legal Aspects in Construction
Heavy Construction Estimating
Soils in Construction
Construction Methods Management

Software

Primavera Project Planner
Lotus 1-2-3

Experience

Project Engineer, Ebert Construction Company, Noblesville, IN
- Interstate 390 Widening Project
- Responsible for internal and subcontractor and pay-letter quantities
- Produced weekly and monthly cost/quantity reports

Assistant Operations Manager, Allen Construction Company, Indianapolis, IN
- Responsible for residential demolition
- Installed concrete footings
- Performed concrete quantity takeoffs

Computer

- Knowledge of C and Pascal programming languages
- Familiar with UNIX, VMS, AOS/VS, and MS-DCS operating systems
- Proficient in WordPerfect, Ventura Publisher, and Hotshot Graphics

References

Provided on Request

Holly Lachman

2560 York Avenue
Hennepin, MN 55410
H.Lachman@xxx.com
612-555-0037

Career Objective

To secure a position as a senior data processing operator, programmer, or systems analyst that lead to increasing responsibility and career advancement.

Summary of Background

Possess extensive experience in operations, access control, and use of mainframes, telecommunications, and new system installation.

Work History

Senior Data Processing Operator
Pratt-Whitney Aircraft—Hennepin County, MN
January 1991 to present

- IBM School on IBM 3851 Installation and Recovery at IBM Chicago Training Center
- IBM School on MV-MSS Internal Operations and Recovery at IBM Chicago Training Center
- VS Wang Systems Administrator at Wang Des Peres Center
- Management skills courses in customer satisfaction
- PC Operations
- ACF-2, RASF, REXX, security systems access
- NT-70 operation

Environments with which I have had direct operational experience:

- All models of the IBM 3090 series running under MVS/XA and MVS/ESA
- IBM's IMS and CICS operating environments including all transaction and database recovery procedures
- Wang Corporations VMS/VS 2000 series and VS/65 OSE processors
- Texas Instruments microprocessor TI-99/4A
- Word processing systems

Work History (cont.)
Other environments with which I have experience:

- IBM's Professional Office Systems (PROFS)
- All IBM and Control Data Corporation Disk Drives
- Control Data Corporation's Disk Systems
- UCC-7 Scheduling and Production Control System

Other training received includes:

- Effective Memo Writing
- Effective Listening
- Ethical Decision Making

Programmer/Operator Training

- Programming and Operating NCR 500
- Understanding NEAT-3 Programming Language
- Programming and Operations NCR 392

Education
- University of St. Thomas (Houston, TX)
- IDPI 400 Hours E.A.M. Class
- IDPI 400 Hours E.D.P. 1401 SPS and 1401 Autocoder Programming

References will be furnished on request.

Bradley Q. Trapp

1726 Willow Springs • Blue Springs, MD 64015
Brad.Trapp@xxx.com • 816-555-9997

Objective

Senior Executive - Construction/Engineering

Summary

- Executive with diversified construction contract management achievements in a variety of industrial, refinery, petrochemical, and power generation projects.
- Demonstrated ability to contribute to profitable operation and growth in accordance with short- and long-term goals.
- A leader with innovative, analytical, and communication skills, with dynamic results in cost-sensitive processes and special projects.

Professional Experience

Divisional Vice President of Sales, 1995 - Present
Lambert Sky Supply Inc., Blue Springs, MD

- Complete profit and loss and operational responsibility for division of this equipment leasing company.
- Created and implemented strategic business plan for company operations throughout west-central United States (20 states), resulting in the development of 50 new accounts.
- Increased utilization and occupancy rate of company properties from 50 to 95 percent during a five-year period.
- Increased overall revenues by 25 percent from 1997 - 1999.

Executive Manager, 1992 - 1995
Reasoner Inc., White Plains, IA

- Developed a professional project management program to utilize existing company resources and provide for diversification.
- The program outlines in depth a series of options for owner's use in their building program, from conceptual through start-up phase, providing for increased project utilization and reduced building cost.

1 of 2

Professional Experience (cont.)

Vice President and Director, 1989 - 1992
Public Service Iowa, Cedar Rapids, IA

- Completed operational responsibility for this construction and engineering company.
- Supervised engineering, estimating, and construction of many multimillion-dollar industrial projects.
- Directed overall operations to effect a three-year growth by 100 percent, a total of 50 million dollars.

Vice President Construction

- Developed and implemented administrative and financial controls to effect significant annual savings for construction projects.

Manager of Construction, 1986 - 1989
Western Systems, Tempe, AZ

- Represented this construction company in a joint venture of power plant construction.
- Directed construction of six 500 M.W. power plants throughout the Midwest.
- Created and implemented cost reduction actions for plant construction, which resulted in a 25 percent reduction per megawatt cost as compared to the national average.

Education

B.S. Civil Engineering - Michigan State University. 1986

References

Available upon request

Leileihua Puni

678 Kala Kea Place
Honolulu, HI 96817
L.Puni@xxx.com
808-555-9876

Objective

Senior mechanical engineering position with a major corporation engaged in advanced aircraft research and development.

Experience

Technical and manufacturing problem-solving experience for major aerospace firm. Test and evaluation training.

ATT Aerospace Engineering Inc., 7/89 to present

Flight Test Engineer, Structural Loads and Dynamics

- Supervised a test program to demonstrate to the Navy the ability of advanced fighter-bomber aircraft to perform on an aircraft carrier with no adverse effects to the structure.

- Implemented extensive research and data analysis during the development of forward-swept wing aircraft including envelope expansion and thermal properties.

- Participated in the feasibility study of in-flight cargo deployment on board cargo delivery aircraft.

- Position involved nationwide travel and contacts in field offices and Navy, Air Force, and NASA installations.

Manufacturing Engineer

- Utilized CAD/CAM equipment to create numerical controlled programs to fabricate aircraft parts.

Experience (cont.)

- Developed operation procedures to manufacture aircraft details and wing, fuselage, and tail assemblies using high-technology manufacturing processes.

- Participated in extensive study to develop and implement new forming dies to create small aircraft parts.

- Successfully implemented laser and optical technology for the construction of aircraft tooling jigs and fixtures.

Education

DePauw University - Greencastle, IN
Received a B.S. in Mechanical Engineering, 1989

Other Formal Training

IBM Corporation Seminars in CAD/CAM and DISPLA

References

Furnished upon request.

TIMOTHY W. MICHAELS

26 Blue Spruce Lane, Apt. 4 • Brookings, SD 57006
T.Michaels@xxx.com • 605-555-2934

OBJECTIVE

To obtain a position in computer software or systems design with interest
in expert systems and object-oriented programming

EDUCATION

South Dakota State University - Brookings, SD
B.S., 2001 Computer Systems Engineering
Interdisciplinary major combining computer science and electrical engineering

EMPLOYMENT

Associate Programmer, 6-01 to Present
Accufact Systems, Inc.

- Working on two projects.
- Designing a C program to download, manipulate, and
  transmit data between IBM mainframes (IBM PS/2 with HLLAPI).
- Designing an expert systems knowledge base to automate
  generation of report files on IBM system.

Technical Support Specialist, 9-00 to 6-01
Academic Information Resources, SDSU

- Isolated and corrected problems on Ethernet and
  AppleTalk lOCdl area networks, and network modem operations.
- Also performed setup and minor repair of terminals,
  microcomputers, and DEC and Sun workstations.

Field Engineering Intern, 6/99 to 9/99
South Dakota Public Services

- Engineered the maintenance and/or replacement of
  overhead and underground power distribution lines.

Microcomputer Consultant, 1-99 to 3-99
Rand Computer Center, SDSU

- Answered questions involving IBM PC and Macintosh microcomputers.

Software Engineering Intern 6-98 to 9/98
South Dakota Star News
• Researched, designed, and implemented modified
payroll system for production departments of newspaper.

COMPUTER SKILLS
Operating Systems: UNIX, Apple Macintosh,
MS-DOS, OS-2

Languages
Pascal, C, C++, COBOL, Ada, Lisp, FORTRAN 68000
Assembly and BASIC, QLP

Expert Systems
VP Expert

IC Design
VLSI System Design, Computer Architecture,
Digital Design Laboratories

HONORS
National Merit Scholarship

Professional Engineers in Private Practice, Western Chapter

REFERENCES
Available

Marcia Rhodes

Present Address:	1624 Stanley • Missoula, Montana 59802 406-555-8532 • Marcia.Rhodes@xxx.com
Permanent Address:	489 Seashore Drive Brownsville, Texas 78521 506-555-0912
Objective:	To obtain a position in information systems, software development, or related field.
Education:	B.S., Computer Science University of Montana Degree expected: June 2004

Experience:

Summer 2003
Texare Oil Company, Houston, TX
Computing Applications Intern

- Converted right-of-way and claims database from hierarchical structure (FOCUS) to relational structure in Database II and developed its user interface.
- Gained familiarity with COBAL, DB3, PL/I, and SQL, database design.
- Responsible for written and oral presentation.

Summer 2002
Texacana Oil Company, Houston, TX
Subsurface Engineering Intern

- Conducted research to evaluate the nature of tubing leaks in gas lift valve and flowing wells in southeast Texas and develop recommendations to reduce their occurrence.
- Involved research project design, use of Statistical Analysis System (SAS), and written and oral presentations.

Additional Information:

Knowledge of Ada, BASIC, C, C++, DB2, Pascal, SQL, Prolog, Smalltalk TSO and UNIX operating system, and Lotus 1-2-3.

Editor, *Environmental Newsletter*, University of Montana.

ROBERTA WEST

1625 WEST 71 STREET • INDIANAPOLIS, IN 46208
R.WEST@XXX.COM • 317-555-6065

OBJECTIVE
> Construction Manager

EXPERIENCE
> Vice President, Commercial Structures Inc.
> Area Manager, Allison Transmission
> Project Manager, Pratt-Whitney
> Senior Estimator, Allison Transmission

SKILLS
Business Development
Contract/Subcontract Administration
Estimating
Scheduling
Claims Preparation/Negotiation
Cost Preparation/Negotiation

EMPLOYMENT
> **Senior Estimator, 8/98 to Present**
> **Gisler Construction Co. Inc.**
> 4456 Grafton Drive, Speedway, IN 46220
> • Estimated highway and bridge projects to 100M dollars.
> • Estimated civil portions of bid packages.
>
> **Project Manager, 1/95 to 8/98**
> **JMM Consulting Engineers, Inc.**
> 334 West 27th Street, Pasadena, CA 76543
> • Completed 55M dollar Cross Lake Bridge for Department of the Army.

EDUCATION
> Northern Illinois University
> DeKalb, Illinois
> B.S. Degree in Industrial Technology

REFERENCES
> Available Upon Request

Daniel Smith
543 Hillside Drive
Palo Alto, CA 94304
Dan.Smith@xxx.com
415-555-9876

Objective:	To apply rigorous quantitative methods and models to strategic planning issues.
Education:	Columbia School of Engineering and Applied Science B.S. in Operations Research Concentration: Computer Science Degree Expected: June 2004 **Courses Taken:** • Mathematical Programming • Data Structures and Algorithms • Accounting and Finance • Production-Inventory Planning and Control
Computer Skills:	**Languages:** BASIC, C, FORTRAN, Pascal **Hardware:** DEC-29, Sun Workstation, IBM, and Macintosh **Software:** Lotus 1-2-3, various business software **Operating Systems:** Tops-20, UNIX, DOS
Experience:	Research Assistant to Professor Samuel Silvers Department of Operations Research Columbia University, New York, NY • Developed and implemented performance analysis of scheduling • Designed scheduling system for University laboratories
References:	Available

Chapter 6

Sample Cover Letters

This chapter contains many sample cover letters for people pursuing a wide variety of jobs and careers in high-tech fields, or who have had experience in these fields in the past.

There are many different styles of cover letters in terms of layout, level of formality, and presentation of information. These samples also represent people with varying amounts of education and work experience. Choose one cover letter or borrow elements from several different cover letters to help you construct your own.

October 18, 20—

Compugraphics, Inc.
8825 North Woodland Drive
Council Bluffs, Iowa 51503

Dear Personnel Director:

I am writing to inquire about any openings you may have for AutoCAD positions. My experience in this field includes part-time AutoCAD work and courses taken covering both AutoCAD and board drafting. I am currently enrolled in the drafting/CAD program at Iowa Vocational Technical College, and I will graduate next month with honors.

I have been a computer operator for the past twelve years, and I am now taking steps toward a career change. I believe my skills and ability to learn quickly will make for an easy transition.

If you have an interest in talking with me further, please contact me. My resume is enclosed for your review. Thank you for your time and consideration.

Sincerely,

David Allen Gisler
5578 Douglas Drive
Council Bluffs, Iowa 51504
(712) 555-9673

ELIZABETH A. GROSSA

1346 E. 22ND ST. #105 • CARBONDALE, IL 62901
(217) 555-9142

May 26, 20—

Box 279
Indianapolis Star
457 Martindale Road
Indianapolis, IN 46227

APPLICATION FOR STRUCTURAL ENGINEERING POSITION

This letter is in response to the ad placed in this Sunday's edition of the *Indianapolis Star*.

I graduate with my B.S. degree in Structural Engineering from Southern Illinois University this coming August. During my time at Southern Illinois, I have specialized in the fields of structural integrity and finite elements analysis. I possess all the skills and education needed to fill the Structural Engineering position. The ad was of particular interest to me, as the job also included some customer and sales interaction.

Enclosed is my resume detailing my work experience and educational background. I feel that my qualifications would be an asset to your organization, and I would welcome the opportunity to meet with you to discuss my experience and qualifications. Please feel free to call me at (217) 555-9142 if you have any questions.

Sincerely,

Elizabeth A. Grossa

Max Power
666 High Drive
New Brunswick, NJ 08901
(908) 555-4958

May 8, 20—

Dear Sir/Madam:

I am inquiring as to whether Greene & Herky has an opening in the area of waste management. I am currently seeking a full-time position, and I am confident that I would be a good fit at your company.

I have completed all my coursework for a master's degree at Harvard University, and I am presently completing my research project: "Safe Ways of Disposing of Solid and Hazardous Waste." My skill in waste management includes knowledge of sound environmental engineering principles that I have acquired both in school and on the job.

Through my experience in real estate development, I learned to deal effectively with senior engineers, colleagues, contractors, and supervisors. I am sincere and dedicated, and I learn quickly. I enjoy challenging work and am capable of working under pressure. Is there a way that I can put these qualities to work for your organization?

I have enclosed my resume for your reference. Thank you for taking the time to consider my qualifications, and I look forward to hearing from you soon.

Sincerely,

Max Power

Michael Eberts

2234 Eden Hollow Road, Suite 5 • Hayward, CA 94545

M.Eberts@xxx.com • Office: (310) 555-8857 • Fax: (310) 555-5959

April 27, 20—

John Boyd
Dodd Engineering
7722 Oakwood Drive, Suite 23
Indianapolis, IN 46250

Dear Mr. Boyd:

The Civil Engineering industry is of great interest to me. I've researched your company and found it to be a leader in the Midwest. I feel that my years of experience could be an asset to Dodd Engineering.

My family and I are planning to relocate to Indianapolis in June; therefore, I am contacting you to inquire about possible employment with Dodd Engineering. The enclosed resume details my extensive experience in architectural drafting and electronics design.

If you feel my strengths could fit within Dodd Engineering, it would be my pleasure to meet with you and share my references and portfolio for your review. I plan to be in Indianapolis late next month if you would like to schedule a meeting. Thank you for your time and consideration. Please keep all contact personal and confidential.

Sincerely,

Michael K. Eberts

January 2, 20—

Mr. William Flick
Lein Engineering
7452 Carmel Drive, Suite 23
Indianapolis, IN 46227

Dear Mr. Flick:

I am seeking an entry-level civil engineering position where I may utilize my educational background to gain professional experience.

I received a bachelor's degree in civil engineering from Purdue University, where I have also completed approximately two-thirds of the requisite credits for a master's degree in civil engineering. I expect to complete my graduate education early next year. In addition, I recently passed the E.I.T. exam with a score in the top ten percent.

While my education emphasizes my career goal of structural analysis and design, at this time I am willing to work in other related fields if necessary.

My resume is enclosed for your consideration. I would appreciate an opportunity to present my qualifications in person. I will follow up by phone next week to discuss your current needs and the possibility of setting up an interview.

Sincerely,

Arlen Bishop
P.O. Box 898
Purdue University
West Lafayette, IN 47907
(317) 555-6978

Louise M. Paugh
1624 Sawbridge Drive
Linden, NJ 07036
L.Paugh@xxx.com
908-555-7546

June 17, 20—

Mr. Andrew Scaruffi
Human Resources
Integrated Environmental Services, Inc.
949 Industrial Drive
Linden, NJ 07036

Dear Mr. Scaruffi:

Thank you for phoning today to discuss your need for an AutoCAD operator. The requirements of the position you describe closely match my experience and abilities. My resume, which offers further details, is enclosed for your review.

I look forward to hearing from you next week after you have had an opportunity to consider my credentials. Perhaps we can arrange an interview in person, as I am interested in learning more about the work you do at Integrated Environmental Services.

Thank you for your time and consideration. If you have any questions, please feel free to call me at (908) 555-7546.

Sincerely,

Louise M. Paugh

RUSSELL GREEN

4848 W. Farris Street #234   Indianapolis, IN 46220

Telephone: (317) 555-9876   E-mail: Russ.Green@xxx.com

September 23, 20—

Human Resources
Environmental Design Inc.
6225 Maple Station
Indianapolis, IN 46220

Attention: Director of Human Resources

This letter is in response to the advertisement that appeared in the *Indianapolis News* on September 22 for a CAD designer. Please accept the enclosed resume in consideration for the position.

In addition to the extensive education I received at the University of Wisconsin, I have five years of work experience in CAD. I feel that my education in combination with my current use of CAD would enable to me to make a valuable contribution as a member of your staff.

Please feel free to contact me at the phone number or E-mail address listed above. I appreciate your time and look forward to hearing from you soon.

Sincerely,

Russell Green

Steven R. Kohlhase
473 Hill Drive West • Kenosha, WI 53143 • (414) 555-6320

June 17, 20—

Mr. Richard Tolbert
Alistates Engineering
6341 Crestwood Dr., Suite 416
Naperville, IL 60665

Dear Mr. Tolbert,

Given your company's excellent reputation in environmental engineering, hydrogeology, and solid waste, your firm must appreciate the need for polished, professional business writing for all the project reports Alistates Engineering submits. My education in environmental science and my current work experience as a technical writer/editor with an engineering firm have given me the knowledge and solid writing skills that can benefit a firm like Alistates Engineering.

In addition to writing, my enclosed resume outlines my extensive background in public affairs. Also, you will notice, my coursework in environmental chemistry, geology, and systems analysis has provided a strong foundation for my career focus on environmental writing. I am very familiar with reading blueprints and reviewing cost estimates, change orders, and bidding procedures. I am diligent and consistently meet publishing deadlines. In addition, I am a skilled electronics technician.

Because proven ability and skills are best evaluated in person, I would appreciate a chance to meet with you. I look forward to discussing my qualifications with you further. Thank you for your time and your consideration.

Respectfully yours,

Steven R. Kohlhase

Anthony H. Cohen

167 Tuxedo Drive
Redding, CT 06896
(203) 555-1678

February 8, 20—

Mr. George Smart, Director of Telecommunications
Compu-Phone Inc.
Lestor Street, Suite 4A
Virginia Beach, VA 23456

Dear Mr. Smart:

As I plan to leave behind a rewarding ten-year career with AT&T, I am antic-
ipating a new and rewarding challenge. I am seeking a new challenge in which
my managerial and technical capabilities can be beneficial.

During my career at AT&T, I've held the positions of engineering manager,
director of operations, and director of data control. Being part of the communications industry has taught me the importance of providing fast, accurate, and reliable service to the organization and its clients.

I would like the opportunity to speak with you concerning my broad background and skills. I feel that my abilities would be an asset to Compu-Phone.
I will follow up next week, after you have had an opportunity to review the
enclosed resume, to discuss the possibility of an interview.

Sincerely,

Anthony H. Cohen

AHC/tbd
Enclosure

FELICITAS A. FINNER

55778 Ventura Boulevard • Encino, CA 91319
415-555-9466 • F.Finner@xxx.com

July 2, 20—

Mr. David Mendoza
Director, Human Resources
Cimflex Corporation
P.O. Box 887
Topeka, KS 66608

Dear Mr. Mendoza:

Thank you for speaking to me by phone this afternoon. As you know, I am pursuing a career in robotics and would like to learn more about Cimflex Corporation.

This May, I graduated from Indiana University with a bachelor's degree with honors in robotic engineering. My current internship with Econtron Engineering has offered me valuable exposure to the operations of a consulting firm involved in the robotics field.

The enclosed resume should assist you in evaluating my qualifications. If you have any questions, please feel free to contact me at the number listed above. I look forward to meeting with you to discuss my qualifications for employment with your company. Thank you for your consideration.

Sincerely,

Felicitas A. Finner

Enclosure

• GORDON EXTINE •

2556 Broadlawn Street • Houston, TX 88674

May 27, 20—

Personnel Director
Dimetrics Inc.
P.O. Box 788964
San Francisco, CA 94147

Dear Personnel Director:

I would like to be considered for the environmental position with Dimetrics Inc. that was advertised on the Internet. I graduated from Notre Dame with a B.S. in Public Affairs with a major in Environmental Science and Affairs.

I feel that my experience in the field of environmental science as a student assistant in the science department, along with my education, qualifies me for a position with your firm. I hope to continue my success as an environmental scientist with your company.

I would like to have a chance to speak with you and discuss how my placement with your firm would benefit both of us. Please feel free to phone me at (218) 555-8866. I look forward to hearing from you.

Sincerely,

Gordon Extine

Jerry Glick
5544 Wildwood Drive • West Lake, Ohio 44145
J.Glick@xxx.com • (314) 555-7866

March 17, 20—

Robotics and Automation Control Inc.
255 Long Hill Rd.
Middletown, CT 06457
Attention Joe Osel

Dear Mr. Osel,

I wish to apply for a position as an Automation Engineer in your company. I graduated with an environmental chemistry degree and have worked with four companies specializing in environmental consulting. My extensive and varied background working with the environment, combined with my schooling and personal enthusiasm, could prove very valuable to your firm.

I have enclosed my resume for your review. I look forward to hearing from you and hope that we can schedule an interview at your convenience.

Sincerely,

Jerry Glick

VICTOR A. GONZALEZ

1990 East Lake Ave.
Lincolnwood, IL 60646

March 16, 20—

Human Resources Director
Elite Engineering
8825 North Woodland Drive
Council Bluffs, Iowa 51503

HR Director:

I am writing to inquire about any openings you may have for positions involving construction management. My experience in this field includes a part-time research position and courses covering both engineering economics and civil engineering materials. I am currently enrolled in the civil engineering program at Iowa State College from which I expect to graduate next month. I have been a computer operator for the past 12 years and am now seeking a career change through re-education and enhanced skills.

My resume is enclosed for your review. If you need any other information to evaluate my credentials for a position with your firm, please feel free to call me at (847) 555-8367. I appreciate your time and consideration.

Sincerely,

Victor A. Gonzalez

MARIA P. DAY
3345 Tenth Street
West Lafayette, IN 47906

April 17, 20—

Personnel Director
Quad System
456 Lindenwood Ave.
Austin, TX 78746

Dear Personnel Director:

I am writing to obtain further information regarding possible employment with Quad System in the area of industrial hygiene. I read about your company in *The Texan State Journal* and would like to find out more about your contribution to the field.

I will be graduating from Northwestern University in May of this year with a Bachelor of Science degree in Industrial Hygiene. Throughout my collegiate career, I have maintained a balanced background of activities and academics. In addition, summer internships provided me with invaluable work experience in monitoring techniques and worker relations.

A copy of my resume is enclosed for your review. If you need further information, I will be more than happy to provide you with the necessary materials.

I know how busy you must be during this time of year, but I would appreciate any information you could provide for me. I may be reached at the above address or by calling (409) 555-2203. Thank you and I look forward to hearing from you about my future with Quad System.

Sincerely,

Maria P. Day

Enclosure: Resume

MARGARET STURM
3033 Maple Drive
Minneapolis, MN 55410
(612) 555-1881

May 15, 20—

Human Resources
TNT Engineering
5892 Burlington Station, Suite 995
Indianapolis, IN 46256

Dear Sir/Madam,

I am presently a graduate student at the Krannert Graduate School of Management, Purdue University where I am working toward my degree. I will graduate with a Master of Science in Industrial Administration (MSIA) this June.

As my prior educational background and work experience are in architecture design and management, I was provided with a profile of your company by the staff of the Krannert Graduate School of Management Placement Office.

I was impressed by what I read about TNT Engineering, especially your significant growth during the past five years and your environmentally friendly policies. I would be pleased to find a position with your firm.

To that end, I am enclosing my resume for your review. If you need any additional information, please let me know. I look forward to hearing more about current openings at TNT.

Sincerely,

Margaret Sturm

Enclosure

David Ott
2468 Raymond Avenue
Clear Lake, Iowa 51504
October 5, 20—

Dear Colleagues:

I am a graduate of Stanford University with a B.S. in biology. I am interested in a position with your firm dealing with wetlands water quality and/or biomonitoring duties. I have experience with wetland delineation, plant taxonomy, and federal and state laws dealing with wetlands and waterways.

My most recent experience with wetlands and biomonitoring was with WPR Energy. My wetland duties included delineation of wetlands on WPR Energy land holdings, work on proposed transmission line rights-of-way, and advising on wetland restoration.

I have personally pursued wetland and waterway violations in Illinois and have experience dealing with the Illinois Department of Natural Resources, EPA, and Corp of Engineers on all the above topics.

I am a self-motivated and professional worker, and feel I could make a contribution to your firm. I would appreciate it if you would keep my name on file for any possible openings.

Sincerely,

David Ott

Miles Edmonds
5328 Jefferson Street
St. Louis, MO 63119
314-555-0598
M.Edmonds@xxx.com

June 16, 20—

Mr. Carl Edelfelt, President
Edelfelt Environmental Testing Services
8784 Scott Street
Palo Alto, CA 94304

Dear Mr. Edelfelt:

I recently learned from the vice president of your company, Susan Satterfield, of your need for an air quality electronics technician. I hope you will agree that my skills and experience match your firm's current needs.

As my resume indicates, I am currently an air quality electronics technician for the state of Missouri. Although I enjoy my current job, I am always looking for an opportunity for professional growth. I am also willing to relocate.

I will be in Palo Alto from May 20 to May 27, and I would like to arrange an interview during that time. I will call your office early next week to make arrangements. Thank you for considering my credentials.

Sincerely,

Miles Edmonds

John P. Whitehead

March 25, 20—

57 Larchmont Road
Wilkes-Barre, PA 18711
(717) 555-6979

Seattle Services
Human Resources
635 Industrial Drive, Suite 248
Wilkes-Barre, PA 18711

Human Resources,

I am interested in applying for full-time employment as an interior designer/facility planner in the Pennsylvania area. As you can see from my resume, I have a strong concentration in design concept, construction documents, project management, and computer-aided design (CAD).

During my time at Penn State, I have had three high-profile internships that have equipped me with additional design, administration, and management knowledge. My combined education and working internships have taught me valuable skills that I am ready to utilize in a full-time position at Seattle Services.

I would like the opportunity to meet with you to discuss my resume and present my portfolio. I believe that I could be a productive addition to your company. If you have any questions, please feel free to call me at (717) 555-6979. Thank you for your time and consideration.

Sincerely,

John P. Whitehead

Paul F. Johnson

516 North Central Ave.
Indianapolis, IN 46208
Paul.Johnson@xxx.com
317-555-8483

June 3, 20—

Mr. James Day
Frankes Engineering
9888 West Washington Blvd.
Monterey Park, CA 91754

Dear Mr. Day:

This letter is in reply to the advertisement for a civil engineer posted in this Sunday's *Indianapolis Star*.

I recently earned a B.S. in civil engineering from Purdue University. I specialized in the fields of construction inspection/engineering and land surveying. I have attached a qualifications summary and other pertinent data for your consideration.

I believe that your firm could utilize my education and dedication as a civil engineer. I look forward to speaking with you further concerning Frankes Engineering. Thank you for your consideration.

Sincerely,

Paul F. Johnson